PSYCHOANALYSIS
AND
REVOLUTION

PSYCHOANALYSIS AND REVOLUTION

Critical Psychology
for Liberation Movements

Ian Parker
and
David Pavón-Cuéllar

1968 Press

First published 2021 by 1968 Press. 2nd Printing.

ISBN: 978-1-9196019-0-8 (pbk)
ISBN: 978-1-9196019-1-5 (ebk)

Printed by Clays Ltd., Bungay

1968 Press
London

CONTENTS

My writing this preface for *Psychoanalysis and Revolution*
is simultaneously the preface of my own journey as a
Black feminist psychoanalytic activist. Very early in my
forty years of Black queer feminist activism, I gravitated
to psychoanalysis because I desperately needed a way of
understanding my own and others' subjective responses
to intersectional racist patriarchal capitalism. However,
bringing psychoanalysis and revolution together does
not make for an easy life because of a constructed binary
where you are meant to be in the psychoanalytic camp
or the revolutionary camp. This binary has never made
sense to me in my activist work for the radical transformation of the existing orders of racist patriarchal capitalism.
    The questions, contradictions, and tensions that
Ian Parker and David Pavón-Cuéllar grapple with in this
book are the frictions I grapple with in sustaining intersectional anti-capitalist hypervigilance of psychoanalysis
and ideas of liberation. Just as Parker and Pavón-Cuéllar
argue, I have learned to inhabit these tensions as a site
of productive subversion. For example, I am habitu-
ated to the tension of feeling alienated within liberation

movements and psychoanalytic communities of practice that both use discourses of counter-alienation. A
contradictory position of relying on frameworks of
anti-alienation, whilst feeling alienated within and by
them. However, in agreement with Parker and Pavón-Cuéllar, I believe the impossibility of psychoanalysis
as revolution is its possibility—indeed its imperative.

Those of us, working for liberation from intersectional oppression, know that it is not enough to tackle
external social structures of domination without tackling
our subjective structures of domination. The matrix of
domination is at once inside and outside of me, you, us.
Revolution to overthrow the matrix of domination rests
on holding an 'at once' insider/outsider analysis. What is
required is critical psychology for liberation movements.
To be clear, critical psychology '*for*' liberation movements,
where the '*for*' functions as 'a bolt on', or 'an addition to',
will fail because any 'bolt on' is repetition of division and
all movements for liberation contest divisions. So, the
task, and it is the task of this book, is of finding ways to
think, feel and work with the psychic life of power that
are manifest and repeated within the mission for revolution. Movements of liberation need to know what they
want liberation from.

The task of breaking chains that can be seen and
are tangible is only a part or dimension of the task. We
are all bound by invisible and intangible chains, which
psychoanalytic jargon calls the unconscious. The question that Parker and Pavón-Cuéllar work with is: how
does an implicated unconscious that is 'structured by
the particular languages we learn from the world in
which we live' form a 'revolutionary subjectivity', or
'revolutionary subject'? The question is crucial to solidarity for revolution. All movements for liberation

rest on a sense of collective solidarity. However, as the Combahee River Collective teaches us, the effectiveness or success of any manifesto of revolution correlates with effectiveness or success of relating across intersectional differences as equals. For example, the effectiveness or success of the Black feminist revolutionary anti-border manifesto of intersectionality would be gravely constrained if it were only applied to visible, tangible structural vectors of oppression.

The effectiveness of Black feminist collective solidarity correlates with the extent to which I, you, we uncover and transform our internal borders or the anti-intersectional in each of us. Our capacity for subjective hospitality across our differences will determine the extent and shape of revolution and liberation. Whether it is in the context of collective meetings for revolution, clinical settings of the therapy room, the context of a helpline call, a protest march or vigil, we must find ways of exploring and transforming power-unequal dynamics between us to transform unequal power dynamics structurally. The Black queer feminist and revolutionary Audre Lorde tells us that the focus of revolutionary change is never just the oppressive situations we want to change, but is also the oppressor's tactics and relationships which are planted deep within all of us. In short, we cannot rely on shared goals or contexts of revolutionary activism to facilitate excruciatingly uncomfortable scrutiny of power, privilege, and position functioning subjectively between us.

As a Black feminist revolutionary group analyst, for me psychoanalysis remains instrumental in revealing the preface (Latin root *praefātiō*) of my revolutionary subjectivity. It is, as Parker and Pavón-Cuéllar state, that 'we must take seriously what brings us back to where we started, what stops us or drags us back'. The prefaces or 'saying (*fātiō*) beforehand (*prae*)' of our journeys are inevitably intimately different, but the revolutionary subject Angela Davis tells us that the saying beforehand of our stories or prefaces never unfold in isolation.

As reader(s) you will find your own positions of solidarity and responses to Parker and Pavón-Cuéllar's manifesto *Psychoanalysis and Revolution*. As revolutionary activist reader(s) you will find questions and demands that will speak to the task of how we stitch our subjectivity prefaces to form a revolutionary ideological quilt—here points of disagreement are as important as agreement.

I have read and will continue to re-read this manifesto and take the liberty in this preface to offer my own interpretation of Parker and Pavón-Cuéllar's four demands:

1.   The unconscious is intersectional. We must develop a Black feminist lens on psychoanalysis to enable our intersectional unconscious to be a location and collective resource of intersectional struggle for Black feminist eco-socialist liberation.

2.   *Repetition* inside and outside all contexts of revolutionary activism, including the clinic/therapy spaces is the opportunity for relating across our differences as equals. Historical amnesia is divisive and must be countered by critical remembering.

3.   Learn from Black feminism that silence does not protect and the first step to eco-socialist liberation is speaking truth to power.

4.   The location of interpretation is the location of power; therefore, in ideological practices, such as psychoanalysis, which explicitly use interpretation as a tool, it is the person in analysis who makes the interpretation to realise their power and undo the power of the psychoanalyst—a vital step in decolonising transference.

Suryia Nayak

AUTHORS'
PREFACE

This manifesto is for movements of liberation, for a better world. It is written for and addressed to individuals and groups that fight against the oppressive, exploitative and alienating reality of our time. It is about the interrelationship between this miserable external reality of life today and our 'internal' lives, what can be called our 'psychology', that which feels to be deep down 'within us', that seems to be either too-often resigning itself to reality or, we hope, rebelling against it. We need to rebel, for the sake of others and for ourselves.

Sometimes we feel that our own rebellion cannot come out from within us, find release, and turn into action. It is as if it were something that eats away inside us which may seriously affect our lives. We may then be told that we have a psychological disorder.

Many problems are reduced to the level of individual psychology by society, by mass culture and by professionals trained to do exactly that: psychologists, psychiatrists and other 'psy' professionals. The problems do feel to be 'psychological', but they are not. How should we politicise them? How can we fight 'outside' against the roots of what we feel 'inside'?

The relationship between the personal 'inner' and the social 'outer' world is crucial for liberation

movements. That is why these movements can benefit from psychoanalysis developed first as a clinical approach that has spent more than a century grasping the
intimate interconnection between reality and what feels
deep within each of us. We must understand the nature
of that interconnection, with the help of different approaches, including those from psychoanalysis. We do
this in order to fight against what oppresses us, exploits
and alienates us, but also to build a practical alternative to
capitalism, sexism, racism and new forms of colonialism.

Psychoanalysis

What is psychoanalysis? Psychoanalysis is a therapeutic
practice that was invented by Sigmund Freud in Europe
at the end of the nineteenth century as an alternative to
mainstream medical psychiatric approaches to distress.
Instead of subjecting people in distress to incarceration,
terrible physical treatments and drugs, the psychoanalyst meets their client or patient, the one that we term
'analysand', in their clinic. Their task is to *listen* to this
speaking subject, providing a strange confidential space
for this analysand to speak of their distress and to hear
connections made between past and present in their own
speech, connections that they have never heard before.

The classic images in popular film of the
analysand lying on a couch in the clinic are true, but
there is something misleading in the images of the psychoanalyst taking notes and issuing a diagnosis and giving wise interpretations. Psychoanalysis opens a space

for the analysand as speaking subject to eventually give interpretations that strike them as true, and that then operate as the motor of 'insight' and change. Psychoanalysis can enable an analysand to simply address the 'symptom' that brings them to see the psychoanalyst, or it can be life-changing. We are modest in our claims for psychoanalysis in this manifesto, but we do believe that it is a progressive therapeutic alternative to psychiatry and psychology, and we will explain why.

We will describe crucial elements of psychoanalysis in the following chapters, focusing on the notion of the *unconscious*, showing how our lives unconsciously repeat patterns that are then repeated in the clinic; we show how this *repetition* of sometimes self-defeating and painful patterns is an expression of a *drive* that can operate for life or for death, and how this repetition is handled by the psychoanalyst in the clinic as *transference*. We insist on the clinical grounding of these four elements because psychoanalysis has emerged and developed as a clinical method, not because we seek to promote psychoanalytic treatment or recommend it to our readers. Rather, our purpose is to highlight what we consider potentially revolutionary in psychoanalysis and how it serves the liberation movements in their current struggles.

Our interest here is in the progressive and revolutionary political effectiveness of psychoanalysis, and not in the dissemination of psychoanalytic theory or clinical practice, though we do include discussion about the articulation of the 'clinic' as a potentially progressive space with political practice. This manifesto is not another introduction to psychoanalysis, another among many others, but it is an argument for the link between psychoanalysis and revolution. Our readers can read more about the method and the theory in other introductory texts if they wish, but bearing in mind our warnings about the way that psychoanalysis has been adapted and distorted.

Another world is possible, and psychoanalysis is one valuable tool we need now to make that happen. Using psychoanalysis as such a tool does not mean importing psychoanalytic ideology into our forms of struggle or imagining it will always be with us. Psychoanalysis came into being in a particular form that we can make work for us, and it will disappear when its work is done.

Our task in this manifesto is to reconstruct psychoanalysis as an authentic 'critical psychology' and as an effective resource for liberation movements. You will see that we are very critical of psychology as such, as we are of all of the psy professions. Psychoanalysis understood dialectically, acknowledging its faults and emphasising its strengths, takes us way beyond those other approaches.

Our conviction is that psychoanalysis must criticize and transform itself in order to be useful to the liberation movements. Thinking about the specific needs of these movements, we examine here the role of the unconscious, repetition, drive and transference in clinical and political analysis and practice in order to address questions of subjective change and transformations of reality. Although we will not avoid theoretical questions, it is *practice* that is the key, and what we can learn from psychoanalytic clinical practice connects with the practice of liberation.

Revolution

The goal of liberation, as conceived by the anti-capitalist, anti-patriarchal, anti-racist and anti-colonial movements, will always be present at the horizon of this manifesto. The following pages are for the liberation movements and were written with them in mind. These movements are against exploitation and oppression, and we stand in solidarity with them. Our psychoanalysis is also attuned to the 'negative', to what is 'anti', to what it is in us that enables us to rebel. And, like these political movements, our psychoanalysis opens up something positive about the nature of the human subject; a capacity to take stock and reflect and change the world, to make it better suited to creativity and transformation.

This manifesto is written at a time of deep political-economic crisis in which the symbolic world we all inhabit as human beings is being perturbed and shaken, and the future worlds we can imagine creating for ourselves are impacted and threatened by enigmatic real material forces that are operating completely out of our control. The fathomless biological substrate of our being, our unknowable nature, erupts into our symbolic universe at times like this, and when it does so, it exacerbates the societal contradictions we are subjected to, contradictions we must understand and overcome if we are to resist and survive. We are weaker when we are more divided in the face of such danger.

A deadly virus, for example, is a threat to all of us in this world, but its arrival shows very clearly that we are not all in this together, not impacted equally. Those in the so-called 'less developed' countries will suffer more, those already suffering from racism will die in greater numbers, and women confined to their homes, if they have them, will be more prone to violent attack. Every oppressed group, those disabled by this society, and those already weakened by it, already sick, will be more likely to die.

This manifesto was written under lockdown, sent backwards and forwards between the authors, and with consultation with comrades around the world. It contains some ideas often considered 'difficult', often avoided for that reason. The ideas are not easily turned into the easy narrative form of popular texts, and you will experience us circling around key ideas to make them clearer. We repeat key claims in a slightly different way at different points in the text to make them clearer still. Every language is written as a form of translation, and now we want you to translate it back into practice.

Most of humanity is in danger under 'shock capitalism' of the sort favoured by neoliberal capitalists because it favours them. This form of capitalism, like the previous ones but to a greater extent, cannot function without the crises that it fosters. Any reason is good excuse to go into crisis mode for those who benefit.

A crisis that erupts from the real is indeed shocking, it shocks us to our core, and it is psychoanalysis that can best grasp the intimate connection between this real, our attempts to imagine what is happening to us, and the symbolic universe we share. Grasping this connection requires an ideology critique that must be linked with what we experience, with what we suffer as subjects, so we can better act to change reality. It is a task for psychoanalysis, but it must be a collective political task, not an individual psychological one.

Our individuality and its psychology are part of the problem. We must question them. We need a particular kind of critique of psychology, a 'critical psychology' that is psychoanalytic. Now we need psychoanalysis.

1

What do *symptoms* tell us about the kind of sick society that intensifies them, in some cases creating them? Everyone under pressure, whether they are workers in the factory, the office, the store, the fields, the streets or the home, needs practical and emotional support at some point in their lives, and all the more so activists struggling to change the world. Activism in liberation movements is often a hard test for people who must break with their past, leave their assigned roles, confront their environment, question themselves, detach themselves from their previous identities and shake themselves from what holds them in their place, give up the privileges that tempt them to cling onto what they already have.

Sometimes our privileges, in the case of the super-rich, the 1%, are massive, but often those privileges that divide us from each other are surprisingly little. It is surprising that being so insignificant they can be so important to us. Their grip is material but also 'psychological', something psychoanalysis understands and can transform.

We must loosen our psychological chains if we are to realise what we are as workers of different kinds. As great as the differences between us are, there is the work we do to live that unites us, and we must recognize that in order to join forces and win the world. We will continue to lose the world, until losing it completely, as long as we remain trapped inside of what we have been forced to be as individuals or trapped inside identity categories handed down to us.

Everyone must liberate not only themselves but be liberated from themselves, the individual selves that are a refuge from a sad world but in which we are also imprisoned. This process causes internal ruptures, even forms of trauma that can be considered, studied and treated. They cannot be completely resolved, but understood, understood and transformed by the psychoanalytic theory and practice of the Viennese medical doctor Sigmund Freud beginning his work at the end of nineteenth century, theory and practice refined and developed by his disciples and followers over the last hundred years.

The history of the Freudian heritage is that of a unique, unparalleled treatment of internal ruptures of modern subjectivity. It is also the history of a complex, ambivalent and contradictory relationship with the ultimate goal of liberation. This history comprises advances, deviations, detours and setbacks. From the beginning, Freud was a child of his time, steeped in sexist and racist ideology and in his own psychiatric training, but he broke from dominant ideas about psychology and human nature to open the way to a more potentially progressive 'critical psychology'.

Freud related critically, sceptically to the psychological sphere. He did not accept it as something given, real and entirely manifest, as something that could be known objectively. Nor did he see it as something unitary that would always be the self-same and the same in every person. All this allowed him to have valuable insights into the human nature of misery as something historical, into the dialectical process through which we can understand that misery as something condensed in *symptoms*, and into the relationship between understanding and liberation.

Symptoms of misery as historical phenomena

What Freud did was to understand what looked like medical symptoms that locked people in place psychologically as 'symptoms' of a very different kind. These 'symptoms' could no longer be explained or treated by medicine, but required other quite different theoretical and practical means. Psychoanalysis was developed by Freud, even though he was trained as a traditional 'mind doctor', in such a way as to break completely from medical psychiatry and from the kinds of psychology that still treat distress within a rather mechanistic medical model. As we will see, unlike the symptoms of medicine, psychoanalytic 'symptoms' are not simply visible signs. They are more like words that demand to be listened to, that *speak*; these symptoms speak of distress and resistance, and they open up possibilities of change.

     The world can be transformed by treating symptoms as psychoanalysis does, by listening to them, taking them seriously, and acting accordingly. Transformative, subversive and potentially revolutionary political action may arise from the symptomatic speech of our suffering, from what cannot continue as it has done, from what must change. That is why such symptoms are our starting point in this manifesto.

3

We are particularly concerned here with the psychoanalytic link between speech and action, political action that tries to address and overcome the most fundamental social causes of our suffering. The pressure and internal ruptures that we suffer from speak of the particular nature of distress in this wretched society that we want so much to change, and psychoanalysis is a potentially powerful ally in that process.

Our task is to connect social struggle with the kind of unavoidable internal struggle described by psychoanalytic theory. The practical purpose is not the usual therapeutic aim of pacifying ourselves, internally reconciling ourselves with ourselves and with society, but the radical political aim of going to the root of our internal struggle. This makes the psychoanalysis that interests us here differ significantly from any psychoanalytically-inspired adaptive individual therapy.

Psychoanalysis, a theory and practice of our torn, divided, 'internal mental lives', has often been allied with power, but it actually provides a clinical and political critique of misery. It is not something to be afraid of. It was not designed to subjugate us by adapting our existence to the established order, by making us distrust our transformative ideals, by turning us away from our collective struggles, by locking ourselves inside our individual minds or by blocking our most intimate resistance against domination.

What Freud has left us is not an instrument of isolation, resignation and subjection. It is true that psychoanalysis sometimes functions like that, as every professional approach to our mental lives has. This is not surprising in class society, which divides professional healers from the rest of the people, assigning them a precise function linked to power.

Psychoanalysis also teaches us that every professional, whether a medical doctor, a psychiatrist or non-medical psychologist or psychotherapist, is also divided, torn by their conflicted lives. They may strive for a successful career but they also sometimes remember what brought them into training to care for others in the first place. We all live those tensions in some way or another, manage them, and usually cover them over. The key question is what we do with those conflicts and contradictions, whether we will make them work for us instead of against us.

Although it has been used in reactionary ways, psychoanalysis is not itself reactionary. It is not necessarily an instrument of domination. On the contrary, it can be a weapon against power. It is possible for it to be used, to show how our own psychology is colonised by reality, this miserable reality of life under capitalism, and how we can speak and act against that individualised psychology as we engage in own liberation.

We are more than what we are told is our 'psychology' by the psy professionals. We are not condemned to shut ourselves up within our individuality or to endure reality or its misery or the capitalist system. We are told that we cannot change things, but we can, and we need an approach that is grounded in the possibility of change.

Adaptation

Psychoanalysis—which is a critical psychological approach to distress and a radical treatment invented at the beginning of the twentieth century—was once explicitly allied to the left. Now it often operates as a tool of *adaptation*. Most psychoanalysts were members or supporters of the communist or socialist movements before their own organisations were destroyed by fascism in Europe and before they fled to different parts of the world. These psychoanalysts had a commitment to changing the world because they could see, and hear from their patients, what misery there was in the world.

The 'symptoms' listened to by the first psychoanalysts were not simple indications of medical organic problems. They were signs of conflict, of conflicts that were not only personal, but ideological, political and historical. The symptoms were themselves conflicts condensed and expressed in language addressed to others, speech. This is the kind of symptom psychoanalysis knows how to listen to.

Many psychoanalysts lost the art of listening. Their listening sometimes gave way to an objectifying and classifying gaze. Psychoanalysis gradually became a medical or psychological speciality. Its practice turned into a simple 'technique' that was purportedly scientific and deliberately depoliticized.

Even the first psychoanalysts, under the hostile conditions in their new host countries to which they had fled, had to renounce political militancy and protect themselves against the anti-communist persecution characteristic of Western countries during the Second World War and then the Cold War. They pretended to be apolitical and thus adapted to their new reality, and they depoliticised and adapted psychoanalysis, turning psychoanalysis itself into an adaptive treatment. This adaptation is crucial to the story of psychoanalysis as a mode of treatment in the clinic and in the place it occupies in popular culture.

The kinds of conflicts that symptoms spoke of were now seen as things to be resolved at a personal level, and politics was kept out of the clinic. Then, when psychoanalytic ideas were mistakenly 'applied' to society, it was this reduced adaptive kind of psychoanalysis that was used as a model for how society functioned and for what any and every society could look like.

During those grim times, and they were grim times for the psychoanalysts as well as for those they treated, it was almost as if the radical history of Freud's innovative theory and practice had died. Some practitioners struggled to keep going, and some social theorists tried to use it in order to grasp the underlying historical conditions that had led it to forget its own past. Almost all of them understood very well, in one way or another, that psychoanalysis had given in, that it had allowed itself to be absorbed and tamed, adapting and becoming adaptive. Now we need to free psychoanalysis from this historical link with adaptation, take its radical authentic historical core seriously, and bring it to life again.

If we must reject adaptive psychoanalysis, it is because this dominant conservative version of psychoanalysis renounces its transformative potential. It does not make it possible for us to transform ourselves, but only to adapt and thus accept and perpetuate reality as it is, however oppressive, exploitative and alienating it may be. Then, although capitalism is unfair and intolerable, we adapt to it as if it were our natural environment, as if it were not historical and therefore surmountable.

The problem of adaptive psychoanalysis is not only that it naturalizes the order of things, making this order seem natural rather than historical, but that it makes us see the world as an external 'environment' separate from each one of us. This prevents us from recognising that we are part of the world, that we are in it and of it and that we can transform it by transforming ourselves, but also transform ourselves by transforming it. We are part of the ecologically-interconnected nature of this world, and connected to each other, responsible for each other as the exploited and oppressed and as comrades in struggle. The world, and other people in it, is not simply an 'environment'; it is more than that, and a more intimate part of our selves.

Every liberation movement learns at some point that there is a crucial difference between an 'environment' and 'ecology', and this difference becomes explicit when they connect their struggle with an ecosocialist understanding of our world. To speak of 'environment' is to speak of the world as something separate from us that we then learn to adjust to or try to dominate, while 'ecology' refers to the intimate interconnection between us and the world. Our lives are linked together in networks of solidarity and political consciousness in such an ecological way that we feel the pain of others in struggle, and know that we will only make this world worse if we try to dominate and exploit others, whether they are fellow human beings or other sentient beings. This ecological consciousness of our link with others is at the heart of psychoanalysis.

As conceived of by psychoanalysis, individuals are not truly alone, isolated and separated from one another. We are part of the lives of others and our actions and words can have fatal consequences for them. Somehow we know that we are as responsible for them as we are for ourselves. Our links are not only 'external'. The others are not only 'outside', around us, but also 'inside', inside each one of us, in what we think, say and do. In our gestures there are traces of others as well as in our words and ideas, and there are also echoes of other voices. Past relationships with others not only reappear in present relationships, but are tied into each of us and make us who we are. The constitution of the individual is social and cultural, but also historical, which makes it incessantly transformative.

Just as the conditions of exploitation, oppression and alienation we face are constructed, historically constructed, and so can be put to an end by us, so our peculiar alienated forms of psychology are products of history and can be changed. This is despite the claims of most psychiatrists, psychologists and psychotherapists, to be working on universal unchanging essential properties of mental life. Their work is actually on extremely variable factors determined by culture, by the historical moment, by existing social relations.

Conservative adaptive psychoanalysts, along with most psy professionals, turn the continually changing historical nature of human existence into something fixed. This is all the more curious and reactionary in present-day society in which everything is changing so fast, where it is indeed as if all that is solid melts into air. We ourselves are forced to be flexible and we learn to exist at each moment in a different way, but the psy professionals fix our existence in place as if it were an object as they study and attempt to treat it, thus betraying what is most radical and transformative about our human nature as such.

Their image of human nature is of it as being not much more than a complicated machine. This is the brute animal as a mere instinctual mechanism which only existed in the imagination of human beings who felt superior when comparing themselves to it. Who would have thought that these same human beings would be finally confused with their degrading representation of the animal? It is as if the old degradation of the animal in contrast to the human being has served to prepare us all for the current degradation of the human being in psychology and in other psy professions, including conservative psychoanalysis.

Radical psychoanalysis, in contrast, teaches us that it is in the nature of human beings to reflect on their social conditions and for us all to continually attempt to transform these conditions and ourselves. We attempt to change and we fail, and it is radical psychoanalysis alongside radical political practice that shows us why we fail, and how we are locked in place by the dominant ideals of society and by the unique biography of each person. We cannot wish away the historical conditions that make us who we are, and neither can we wish away the internal obstacles that bind us to our oppression, that incite us to desire oppression at the same time as we resent it and try to escape it. We may not ever be able to free ourselves entirely from our desire for oppression, but we can know it, discern it when it intervenes, erupts, blocks us, and this knowledge can be the first step towards our liberation.

To desire oppression is a most peculiar thing, one of the painful paradoxes of subjectivity. The easiest thing is to pretend that there is no such paradox, but sooner or later we will stumble upon it and this may compromise our struggle for liberation. Perhaps in the end, responding to our desire, we will create new forms of oppression to replace those from which we liberate ourselves. To avoid this, we must take seriously what brings us back to where we started, what stops us or drags us back. We must take all this seriously not in order to blame the victim of this process as if it were simply psychological and inevitable but in order to understand the contradictory nature of each us as human beings in this wretched world.

History

Psychoanalysis, like Marxism and other theories of power and liberation, came into being at a specific historical period in order to conceptualise, understand and solve a historically-created series of problems. We need to grasp the *history* of psychoanalysis in history itself, and make it ours. Outside the historical context of the last two centuries, psychoanalysis would not make all the sense that it does for us. The same lack of sense would also beset Marxism if we transplanted it to another era.

It is difficult to imagine what slaves wanting to escape their rulers in ancient Rome would have made of Marxist analyses of 'surplus value', the hidden share the capitalist takes from a worker, for example, or of attempts to build revolutionary parties and international associations. The proletariat as industrial wage-labourer did not exist at the time of Spartacus. Freeing oneself from slavery was not the same as freeing oneself from the exploitation of wage labour. That is why Marxism only started to become useful when capitalism itself came into the world as a dominant mode of production. Likewise, the development of the colonial states and imperialism was necessary for there to be a need for anti-colonial and anti-imperialist liberation movements. Each political movement arose to combat particular exploitative or oppressive conditions.

In the case of psychoanalysis, the 'symptoms' of distress it was invented to understand and treat are quite specific to modern society. These symptoms are as historical as is the specific strange Freudian representation of the psyche. What is 'unconscious' is very much tied up with the peculiar form of alienation we suffer from in capitalist modernity.

Alienation in capitalism produces 'inner' conflicts that can be invisible as such, but which are known for their effects, for what they cause or motivate in people, such as their inexplicable suffering, the derangement of their lives, their absurd decisions or their erratic actions, sometimes destructive or self-destructive. All this is evident in current work experience. People are locked into their lives as workers in such a way that they repeat the same kinds of tasks, and their life-experience is then structured in a particular repetitive way that is outside their control.

Workers, everyone who works today, are driven to do so by economic imperatives, and so what it is to be subject to a 'drive' to work and to survive is bound up with capitalism. Capitalist domination shapes the power relations that bind us to each other, but these relations also repeat earlier power relations so that repetition is unconsciously driven and then reappears as what psychoanalysts call 'transference' inside the clinic. We will address each of these issues in the course of this book, and through them show that psychoanalysis grasps the nature of symptoms as indications of distress in this society.

Symptoms have been created in such a way that psychoanalysis, a historical invention, is geared to read them, and it helps us to see them for what they are, as conflicts in personal life and as expressing social conflicts. A particular society and a singular person in this society are what make manifest problems in a symptomatic way. Symptoms are indicators that something is wrong, they are messages about how distress is appearing in each separate subject.

INTRODUCTION

Subjects

We refer to human beings as '*subjects*' here in this manifesto because the term 'individual' is too reduced a term, and it implies that our subjectivity is undivided and separate, isolated, opposed to society and locked in its individuality. A 'subject' is more than the individual, it includes other people, it is open and crossed by the social world, inhabited and divided by the outside as its ecological space of being. The subject is in contradiction with itself and for this reason it can be the source of agency and change, whether that is at the level of an individual person or at the level of a collective political process.

The subject can be a historical agent, but also a victim and a product of history. Events affect us and determine us in different ways that can now be approached through psychoanalysis. Psychoanalytic thinking is one of the most powerful resources available to us to understand and change our experience in modern times. What was happening to us as subjects in late modernity, between the nineteenth and twentieth centuries, suddenly took on, with the development of Freudian theory, a radically new sense. Medical names for our distress were invented, and at the same time psychoanalysis was invented to deal with them, to rebel against what they meant, to transform that distress.

Psychoanalysis is still one of the best means to grasp the nature of our present-day symptoms of misery in life under advanced, neoliberal capitalism, with its associated forms of sexism, racism and colonialism. These psychoanalytic symptoms which operate unconsciously and then find distorted expression in the visible symptoms that the medical doctors and psychologists observe have a deeper connection with our individual biographies and with current conditions of life. Symptoms are historical phenomena in this double sense; they are produced in the personal history of each individual and their overall shape is structured by the kind of society we live in and try to make sense of.

Our past and our world haunt us, make us sick and make us suffer. This is whether we are completely bewitched by ideology and believe that this is the best of all possible worlds, no reason to worry, or whether we are an activist who knows that things are bad and have got to change. Conflict and contradiction bedevil us all, and those conflicts and contradictions reach down inside us, worm their way into us, tear us apart and then take the form of symptoms that can be painful and apparently inexplicable.

Psychoanalysis is dialectical, neither psychology nor psychiatry

The tortuous path of the history of the psychoanalytic approach to subjectivity went alongside the development of psychology understood as a scientific or pseudo-scientific specialty and as a professional and academic discipline. This psychology should not be confused with psychoanalysis. Although it has frequently managed to absorb it, it disagrees with it in its premises, ideas, methods and objectives. Psychology, in fact, is constituted by much of what we try to solve through psychoanalysis. From the psychoanalytic point of view, the psychological sphere is problematic.

Psychology takes shape for us as an illusory, deceptive and even delusional experience, namely, the experience of each of us as an undivided and separate individual who can fully know and control themself as if an object. This unitary self is exactly part of the problem because it leads each person to imagine that they should take responsibility for their unwanted unpleasant feelings and makes them feel all the worse if they feel 'divided', if they sense that there is an unconscious dimension to their lives. Such a division, which affects us all, is recognized by psychoanalysis and denied by psychology. Its denial conceals our alienation and prevents us from resisting what alienates us. It thus contributes to what dominates us as if 'from the inside', to manipulate us and to manage us ideologically.

One key problem we face now is the historical construction of an individual isolated experience that does not correspond to our social existence, cannot recognize itself in our feelings and thoughts, has no power or sense in itself and is therefore vulnerable to domination, manipulation and ideological management. Here is the problem of psychology separated from the collective shared nature of our lives as human beings. It is, at root, a problem of individualism in capitalist society and its psychological manifestations.

Psychology

The discipline of *psychology* is devoted to the maintenance of each individual self as a separate psychological sphere, as the experience of their own personal psychology, like that of each worker isolated from the others. Psychology, the academic professional discipline and the sense of our own individual undivided psychology that the discipline works upon, was formed at the same time as capitalism itself, and it has spread, with capitalism, around the world. The expansion of capital around the world has also been a global dissemination of its psychological devices not only in university and health institutions, but in all spheres of life. Everything tends to be coloured with a psychological tone. This process of psychologization involves mechanisms of atomization, desocialization, depoliticization, dehistorization, pathologization, incrimination of individuals and adaptation to capitalist society.

Yes, we live under global capitalism, under brutal neoliberal capitalism today, but to understand how that capitalism functions we need something more than simply one name for the problem. Psychoanalysis, and not only psychoanalysis, teaches us that it is impossible to speak of life under capitalism, to speak of class, without also speaking of sexism and racism and the manifold other forms of oppression that disable people. Radical psychoanalysis is already 'intersectional', addressing the deep subjective link between different forms of oppression that the different liberation movements have arisen to combat and put an end to.

Freeing ourselves from the oppressive experiences of class, race and sex requires us to combat them 'within' ourselves as well. Here, in the subjective sphere, what is oppressed appears not only as affected, but also as resigned or adapted to oppression. This adaptation, which sustains and perpetuates what oppresses us, is often viewed as 'mental health' by psychologists and psychiatrists.

Closely linked with a psychiatric medical model of distress, psychology has developed worldwide as a psychotherapeutic tool to adapt people to reality instead of enabling them to change it. Psychology picks up most of the historical ideological baggage of medical psychiatry and claims to humanise it, focusing on observable measurable symptoms in the behaviour of its clients instead of symptoms of invisible mental diseases. This shift to behaviour from disease is not much of a step forward, and psychoanalysis shows the limitations of this minimal shift of focus.

Psychoanalysis is not psychiatry. But the medical legacy of psychiatry is still present inside psychology even when psychologists present themselves as more friendly and progressive and 'psychotherapeutic'. We should be clear here that there are important theoretical differences, as well as professional status disputes, between psychiatrists who are medically-trained, psychologists who have their own reduced models of individual behaviour and thinking, and psychotherapists who mix and match whichever approach seems to work best in soothing distress and fitting people back into the world.

At the moment, it is psychologists who are centre-stage with their claims to scientific expertise. They consider themselves to be the most effective and compare their effectiveness with that attributed to psychiatry, psychotherapy and psychoanalytic practice. It would be easier for our task, to argue for the value of psychoanalysis, if psychology did not work. The problem is precisely that it does work; psychology fits very well with exploitative and oppressive social relationships, and it functions very well in adapting people so they keep that kind of world running fairly smoothly. It runs smoothly until there are symptoms, which psychology then uses its supposedly psychotherapeutic skills to sooth.

The spread of psychology around the world and into our everyday lives is bringing about a reduction, contraction and simplification of experience, of the

way we feel, think and speak about ourselves. Our behaviour is more and more similar to that of the simplistic
psychological caricatures of human existence that sur-
round us everywhere. These caricatures are disseminat-
ed by means such as film and television, magazines and
newspapers, bestsellers and self-help manuals, emotional re-education, business coaching, counselling, expert
opinions, social networks and even Pentecostal churches.

The entire cultural realm is saturated with
simplified banal psychological representations, highly
functional for the capitalist system, in which we certainly recognize ourselves. We recognise ourselves in
them, not because they are so faithful that they reflect
us as we really could be, but because they are so powerful that they make us correspond to them, live them
out in what we are at the moment in these miserable
conditions of life.

Psychology is so successful because it manages
to unfold through our existence, confirming it as it is now.
Sometimes this existence seems to materialize concepts
of the great psychological traditions, including those of
the behaviourist, the humanist, and the cognitive disciplinary masters. Consumers have learned, for instance, to
respond to advertising stimuli, to identify with the image
of human nature that is sold to them, to process the infor-
mation required to buy and to surrender to the hidden
drives that push them into consumerism as an ideology
and material practice.

There are even successful psychoanalytic versions
of psychology, just as there are psychoanalytic versions
of psychiatry. We need to beware of these imposters, these
ideological distortions and capitulations to 'normality'
of what should be a radical liberatory approach. Psychoanalysis cannot become psychiatry or psychology

without ceasing to be what it is, losing its usefulness for liberation movements in the process and even becoming harmful to them, not only depoliticizing them by psychologizing or psychiatrizing, but contributing to adapt and subjugate rather than liberate.

It is possible to adulterate and degrade psychoanalysis by making it work like psychology and to help subjects to be what they should be in order to insert themselves most efficiently into capitalism. However, if we want to preserve psychoanalysis for what it really is and can be, we need to separate it from this process, and show how psychoanalysis can enable us to resist it. Psychoanalysis itself, because of the history of adaptation it has been subject to, has become implicated with ideology, but it rebels. It is as if psychoanalysis is itself a symptom of oppression that now can be made to speak, and in the process of speaking well of psychoanalysis we may liberate it and liberate ourselves.

Psychoanalysis is riven by conflict, and it speaks of conflict in its approach to our historically-constructed human nature. It has emerged at a precise historical moment, reflecting the contradictory needs, inclinations, desires and aspirations of the kind of human subject who carries the contradictions of this world deep inside them, and that is why we can also speak of psychoanalysis itself as a symptom.

The psychoanalytic approach not only deals with symptomatic manifestations of the suffering of the subject, but itself is a symptom. It is as contradictory as what it addresses. At the very same moment as we demand of psychoanalysis that it attend to the contradictory nature of life under capitalism, attend to the symptoms that arise today in this society, so we also demand that it must be a reflexive 'critical psychology' able to examine itself; we must analyse what makes psychoanalysis adapt to society and what makes it resist and become something subversive and liberating.

Conflict

As it is with psychoanalysis, so it is with each individual who carries a symptom within themselves. They are beset by *conflict*. Individuals are routinely trapped in harmful oppressive relationships by a particular biographically-distinct pattern of experience, and that is what comes to define who they are. This is what makes them recognisable as the same person to themselves, their family and friends.

What is distinctive about each of us is something unconscious in which we are trapped, something resistant and repetitive, as well as contradictory, conflictive. There is internal conflict which is given shape in the symptom peculiar to each one of us. This symptom can paralyse us and prevent us from transforming ourselves and modifying the relationships that oppress and harm us. Change often happens when something dramatic or traumatic happens to us, breaks us from those unconsciously driven patterns, and social change is one big factor in the spur to individual change.

The process of change and the crystallisation of conflict in the symptom can be understood dialectically. Conflict is what traps us, what immobilizes us, but is at the same time what makes us move to solve it and free ourselves from it. Our movement forward is both driven and hampered by conflict. This makes us move little by little, advance and stumble, changing without changing almost anything, something that is particularly apparent when there is a series of little changes that suddenly lead to a transformation, quantitative incremental changes that prepare the way for a qualitative shift. This happens at the political level when sustained collective struggle leads finally, after years of effort, to new possibilities and new forms of subjectivity appearing. And it happens in the clinic when the symptom manifests itself as an open conflict and calls for a decision about how to go on with life. The symptom is an obstacle but also, dialectically understood, it is an opportunity.

The symptom is an opportunity to change and not just to know ourselves. This is why the symptom should not be eliminated, as psychologists and psychiatrists usually try to do, thus ensuring that nothing is discovered and everything remains the same. In order to discover and transform oneself, one must listen to the symptom with the greatest attention, as is done in psychoanalysis.

People come to a psychoanalyst not because they have symptoms, for everyone in this sick society is beset by symptoms, but when those symptoms become unbearable, when there is an impending shift from quantitative misery to qualitative change of some kind. One of the tasks of clinical psychoanalysis is to direct the treatment in such a way that this qualitative change takes place in the form of opportunity for reflection and decided choice about how to live one's life instead of teetering on the edge of breakdown and despair. Psychoanalysis helps the subject not to be overwhelmed or defeated by what is manifested in the symptom, to overcome it, which is only possible by listening to the symptom and acting accordingly. The symptom is dialectical in nature, and psychoanalysis is a dialectical approach which helps the individual subject take a new course, towards adaptation or liberation.

To be liberating, psychoanalysis must be liberated. It has to be released from what it is not and is not meant to be. It must be purified of the sediment of mystifications, prejudices, malign moral values, dogmas, stereotypes and illusions that have turned it from being a progressive approach into one that is instrumentally useful to capitalism and colonialism and to oppressive gender relations.

Psychoanalysis has been instrumentalised in the successive contexts it has attempted to adapt itself to. These contexts have imbued psychoanalysis with their norms, beliefs, prejudices, and values, requiring it to moderate its radical aims and to compromise. Over the course of its history all kinds of reactionary ideological content were injected into its radical form. That ideological content, which includes poisonous ideas about the essential underlying difference between men and women and their sexuality and their gendered relation to each other, is trapped in the body of psychoanalysis as a form of practice, a practice of speech. This is serious because psychoanalysis is itself a 'talking cure' that shows us how what we say is interconnected with what we do.

The conflicts and contradictions of our class society are inseparable from our speech, as well as from our sexual life, which is also at the centre of psychoanalysis. We will try to explain in the course of this manifesto why this is so, and how it is that psychoanaysis homed in on sexuality precisely because that sexuality was seen as the intimate core of our lives.

We talk about sex, and that is what psychoanalysis is so often known for, but why? If the nuclear family was experienced as the heart of a heartless world when capitalism developed, sexuality was experienced as the most private and secret part of ourselves. But it was not only 'repressed', covered over as something shameful and pushed away as something bad, but incited, demanded of us. It was thus turned into an obsession, as well as our weakest point, an open wound, constantly irritated, which serves to dominate us in a 'heteropatriarchal' logic.

Patriarchy is always 'heteropatriarchy'. It is always 'heteronormative', that is, it makes heterosexuality compulsory as the basis of the intimate social contract at the heart of our globalised world because it enforces the power of men over women and of older men over younger men, and it excludes or barely tolerates different forms of sexuality. This is the case even when patriarchal capitalism uses a distorted version of feminist discourse against the left or turns varieties of sexual preference into a niche market.

Just as patriarchal capitalism can instrumentalize feminism and sexual diversity—absorb and distort these radical ideas and turn them against us—so it can turn psychoanalysis into its instrument to normalize and exploit our sexual lives. Our sexuality, therefore, runs the risk of being conditioned by patriarchal discourse not only in the cultural realm, but also in the psychoanalytic clinical setting. We can purge psychoanalysis of that ideological poison now, enabling it to speak for us and not instead of us or against us.

So, against psychology and psychiatry, and against most forms of psychotherapy, psychoanalysis is a psy profession with a difference. It knows how to listen to us and is not condemned to speak in our place. Therefore, instead of pretending to fix things in place, it treats the symptom of our distress as a message from the subject about their miserable condition and, crucially, about the need for change. In this way, it has the potential to be an invaluable ally of liberation movements. It is, in itself, a dialectical theory and practice of liberation.

Liberation in the clinic and culture

Psychoanalysis has been appropriated by those with power, it is true, but this does not mean that we should let it go, let it fall into their hands. We must, rather, re-appropriate psychoanalysis. In order to do this we need to grasp the dialectical relationship between its clinical work and its ever-changing historical context. The historical conditions which saw the birth of psychoanalysis, of alienation under capitalism, exploitation of life and the oppressive nature of the Western European nuclear family, were precisely the conditions that psychoanalysis aimed to understand and combat. It was in those conditions that sexuality was experienced as traumatic because it was repressed but simultaneously spoken about incessantly, provoked.

The conditions in which psychoanalysis appeared, and the ideological forces at work, entered into psychoanalysis, distorting it. There is no 'pure' non-ideological psychoanalysis, but there can be an ongoing cleansing of its theoretical elaborations, permanent unending purification of its key concepts. The complex dialectical relationship between its clinical form and ideological aspects of the theory can be constantly clarified and transcended in practice. It is a continuous process, always unfinished, of struggle against power, critique of ideology and resistance against psychologization.

Four key concepts of psychoanalysis—*unconscious, repetition, drive* and *transference*—operate as radical formal elements of the theory that allow us to resist the deeply ideological process of psychologisation. These terms have a particular meaning in psychoanalysis, but we aim to make them meaningful here to radicals who are not only seeking to change themselves but also seeking to change the world.

The unconscious, repetition, drive, and transference operate in the world and not just on the psychoanalyst's couch. We must consider these four concepts in the space of dialectical tension between the clinic as a private space of transformational work and our historical context. The four key concepts need to be reconstructed in order to make them thoroughly historical; this, to avoid the trap of 'applying' them to liberation movements and so turning them from guiding revolutionary practices to becoming tools of ideology.

We must understand that our struggles do not need to be interpreted, justified, validated and much less conducted by psychoanalytic concepts. Nor do we intend that these concepts should operate as a universe of meaning that limits and closes the horizon of freedom for which we fight. Our liberation movements must keep their path open and decide their direction and scope as they move forward and expand what they can conceive of and accomplish. They should not be guided by psychoanalysis as if by a fixed point of reference, but they can utilise it as one means among others and transform psychoanalysis as they transform everything else in their confrontation with the conditions in which we live.

We confront particular modern conditions of culture, of capitalism blended with colonialism and its necessary forms of racism and sexism and other ways of pathologising people who are unwilling or unable to adapt to this world as healthy well-behaved productive citizens. Psychoanalysis provides valuable insights into the underlying nature of subjectivity in this global culture, and into the differences that divide the peoples of the world against each other. However, its real contribution lies in the clinic, and the four key concepts, of unconscious, repetition, drive and transference that we discuss in more detail in the following chapters of this manifesto, are grounded in its clinical work.

It is in the clinic that we discover what is beyond us, how we repeat self-destructive relationships, how we are driven to do so, and how the phenomenon of transference as an uncanny relationship with the psychoanalyst operates. These discoveries in the psychoanalytic clinic do not happen outside the dominant cultural universe. They logically feed back into culture, for good or ill, and so we also have something to say about the dangers of 'applying' psychoanalysis beyond the clinic as an inevitable academic distortion of its practice.

Beyond its questionable applications, psychoanalysis needs to be recreated by us as a tool of radical work on subjectivity that is necessary if there is to be a successful overthrow of existing conditions. Dialectically understood, this tool is the result of the theoretical elaborations of Freud and his followers, who enabled us to use it for radical work in the clinic and with liberation movements. What it produces is part of a creative process which enables us to make more. Our name for what it makes possible is 'revolutionary subjectivity', a 'revolutionary subject'.

As in the clinic, so it is in politics; the revolutionary subject appears and disappears, comes into being, forged in struggle, and fades again when its work is done. All this will not turn us into heroic revolutionary individuals, charismatic activists, or battle-hardened leaders. What concerns us is not the formation of leaderships or personalities, but the creation of a collective process of change that anticipates the kind of world we want to build, no more than that.

That will not turn us into psychoanalysts, far from it, and the end result psychoanalysis always aims for is to enable the human subject to kick away the ladder that they have used to reach a new place. The psychoanalytic perspective should not close our horizon. It is an opportunity, not a trap. As we bring an end to the world that creates so much misery we also anticipate the end of psychoanalysis, psychoanalysis as a revolutionary approach that is functioning as a tool and result of that historical process. We begin, in the next chapter, with the *unconscious*.

2

UNCONSCIOUS: ALIENATION, RATIONALITY AND OTHERNESS

Our struggle, wherever it is locally, is international in scope, and every liberation struggle progressively expands its horizons to understand how we are divided and ruled. What is done to us is incomprehensible in a framework focusing only on the immediate local, interpersonal, regional level, or even confined to national context.

Consumerism, unemployment and xenophobia in rich countries, for example, only make sense when we consider misery, low wages and the exploitation of labour in poor countries. Similarly, we need to think about old and new forms of colonialism and imperialism to know what is at stake in racial hatred or terrorist attacks. This is also how the Chilean feminist slogan 'the oppressive state is a male rapist' can help us elucidate not only government repression and violence against women, but also homophobic brutality and violent macho forms of relationship between groups and nations that predominate at the expense of other ways of life or ways of being that are feminized and denigrated.

What happens in the world, even if very far from us, underlies what we say and do. Our everyday words and actions also involve past history, even the most remote, even that of past centuries. History bears us. All of this is present at every moment, limiting us and guiding us in a certain direction, but generally in a way that is not fully conscious to us. This limit and possibility is the *unconscious*.

This chapter is about a fundamental underlying concept in psychoanalysis. The unconscious is brought to life in the clinic, but its effects are felt everywhere in everyday life. We need to grasp the way that the unconscious takes on personal and political form in the alienation that is produced in capitalist society and then how our understanding of that is distorted by 'commonsense', how rationality in this society leads us into the trap of the individual self in which the 'ego' is the master in the house, and how the 'otherness' that haunts us is bound up with language, the very same language we use to convey our suffering to others.

Alienation and commonsense

We are alienated in this miserable world, separated from others, and even from ourselves, and what we are told about our alienation, and told about the unconscious, usually has the ideological effect of covering over the source of the problem, preventing us from seeking the help we need. We need to think differently about the unconscious.

By thinking, reflecting and acting politically on an international scale we come to understand how particular others, of different social groups, nations, cultures, genders and sexualities have been rendered 'other' to us, and how that 'otherness' has worked its way inwards in forms of embedded class privilege and insult, of nationalism, racism and sexism. We are made 'other', even to ourselves in this sad world, and otherness then runs through our experience, our subjectivity, so deep that nature itself, whatever that is exactly, is experienced as alien, strange and threatening. This is an important part of what psychoanalysis names as 'unconscious'. It is something unrecognizable that inhabits our 'external' and 'internal' world. Although it is in our thoughts, it is beyond what we think. It is not what we think. We are each divided, split, other to ourselves.

The unconscious always escapes our thoughts. It is not simply something that is buried and that can be exhumed, thought about, remembered. Rather, it is a form of alienation from our ideas, words, actions and relationships with the world, which are always other than what they seem to be, as if they were separated from us.

Alienation is a form of separation. In strictly psychoanalytic terms it is a doubled form of alienation after our necessary separation from those who brought us into the world and first cared for us. By turning away from them, we turn away from ourselves, we divide ourselves internally, so we can make our way in the world, the world we are 'alienated' in and the language we use to communicate that unease to others. Then the particular cultural-historical alienation in this world redoubles and intensifies our 'original alienation', our internal division, our peculiarly human nature as divided subjects who must communicate with others in order to survive, including about our distress.

In this oppressive and exploitative society our alienation operates through multiple dimensions of separation, which include competition between individuals seeking to sell their labour power, control by our masters of the fruits of our creative labour once we have sold our time to them, anxiety over whether our bodies will carry out the work we must perform for others in order to live, and the drive to exploit the natural world for profit which then appears to us as a hostile force confronting us. Other people, our own creativity, our bodies, and nature as such, are each and all separated from us, and then experienced as threatening. Commonsense tell us that this is universal and natural, but commonsense lies.

Commonsense

There is a difference between the 'common sense' we fight for—the kind of common sense that we build from indigenous knowledge, our creative expertise by experience and practical theoretical analysis—and ideological *commonsense* that is handed down to us or stolen and distorted, used to deskill us. That ideological commonsense is what we are concerned with here. That ideological commonsense systematically frustrates our attempts to grasp the form this alienation takes as something 'other' to us, as something un-conscious. However, despite common sense, the other that alienates us is still there. Something escapes conscious control in this world where economic forces drive us to work for others for their profit, and psychoanalysis has much to say about this aspect of our lives that is always out of our reach, existing as something unconscious to us.

Freud's invention of the unconscious is also, in the process, banalised, turned into popular images of murky depths, of something dark and mysterious, or, in many psychology and psychiatry textbooks, as the bulk of an iceberg of which only the top tip is visible to us. Psychologised psychoanalysis then even tells us to drive this unconscious back underground, to ignore it, to pretend that it has no impact on our lives. That false image of mental 'well-being' and 'happiness' pits the self-conscious 'ego' against the unconscious, wishing it away.

This 'ego' which is so well-known to many popularisers of psychoanalysis and enthusiastic supporters of the psy professions, is often described as the rational core of the self, but this little mechanism of rational individual self-consciousness is not actually the core of who we are at all. We are, after all, as Marx teaches us, an 'ensemble of social relations', and that network of social relationships which defines our collective nature as human beings is the site not of the ego, but of the unconscious.

The unconscious, which is not something obscure hidden in the asocial depths of each one of us, unfolds in the social relationships in which we participate and that constitute us. These relationships evoke others, other past relationships, and are beyond our conscious control, but they decide what we are and what we can control. They shape our self and our self-consciousness.

Our immediate self-consciousness often seems to embrace us, but it cannot save us. It misleads us. It wallows in commonsense ideologies of the self separated from society, making the best of alienation instead of acknowledging it, understanding how it has been produced and enabling us to collectively change the conditions that gave rise to it.

Instead of liberating us from alienation, simple-minded 'self-awareness' reproduces it through the alienating images of our 'ego'. These images of the 'ego' as the core of our selves, as the rational centre of our self-consciousness, reduce our subjectivity to what we believe ourselves to be, each one of us as an individual separated from the others. That way of thinking about it is not the route to a cure, and still less to revolution.

We will not get anywhere, outside of where we already find ourselves, so long as we have not managed to free ourselves from the thought that encloses us within what each one of us already immediately and ideologically seems to be. This thought about ourselves, which is fuelled by commonsense, betrays the otherness that makes us human, turning that otherness into a curse instead of the material grounding of a practical enduring real cure through historical struggle against exploitation and oppression. Our liberation can only be collective and this is why it is not encompassed by the kind of common sense that locks us up in the prison of our 'ego'.

In this commonsensical way of thinking, we are exclusively our particular self. The other infinitely diverse particularities of gender, colour, culture or nationality, among many other dimensions of difference, appear as external, as others to us, even as repulsive or hostile. We do not recognize our collective diversity as shared humanity. Notice also how this image of the self-sufficient ego marginalises 'disabled people', people who are treated as if they are damaged, incomplete. They are 'disabled' by this society that requires normal healthy well-adapted bodies to produce 'surplus value' and also by the commonsense normative image of the ego as autonomous master in the house. Those who fail to function as such masters are often condemned as 'mad'.

Our nature as human beings is thereby denied. We betray our underlying nature in which we are nothing without others. As our intimate relation to others is betrayed, loving relations of solidarity with the pain of others is replaced with hatred and suspicion, and so we fall into a trap.

We are trapped in the temptation of assertive, possessive and competitive individual solutions to the misery pervasive in this capitalist world. The temptation is to be as miserable as this world which is governed by the drive to accumulate goods and make profit from others, and to make the best of it, even to claim we are then 'happy'. When this happens, individual mastery, the isolated 'ego', is pitted against others.

However, even if we turn against humanity, we do not stop being human. The unconscious speaks and thus can connect us with collective action. There is a dialectical twist to this connection, which is that while the individual 'ego' is not the core of each human being, neither is the unconscious, the unconscious in which we connect with each other, and in which we are as an ensemble of social relations. The unconscious is not a 'core' of the self any more than the ego is, and the unconscious, furthermore, is not exactly something essential and inherent in my being, not hidden inside each of us. It is not the unfathomable kernel of what I am. It is something else.

The unconscious, which we assume to be so deep and hidden inside each one of us is, itself, something *outside* that speaks of otherness. It is made of history, economy, society, culture and ideology. It is a space for encounters and disagreements with others, explanations and contradictions that are debated with them, alliances and conflicts between comrades in struggle, persuasion and misunderstanding. It appears in the field of language we share with others.

The unconscious is itself structured by the particular languages we learn from the world in which we live. It comes from the outside, from what we see and hear, from the structure of past and present relationships that resonates and unfolds in the space we inhabit. So it functions as an 'other' discourse, always present if not always noticed. It is simultaneously, dialectically, exterior and interior. It surrounds us and crosses through us. It is inside us precisely because it was, and still is, also outside us, because we are in it, because it is where we are.

We live in the *exteriority* of the unconscious. Here, in this outer structured field of being, it is as if each individual must occupy his or her place, the one that corresponds to him or her, that which distinguishes him or her from the others, and then, as they adapt to society, that which makes him or her coincide with them. The unconscious literally puts us in our place, and, at the same time, it unsettles us, reminds us that we are not only what we imagine ourselves to be, that there is more to us than our little alienated selves reduced to thinking in our ego as if it were our diplomatic representative to the world of others.

We learn from the unconscious that we do not have complete power over what we say, that we do not control the meaning of our words, that we are not the centre of our little worlds of meaning or of immediate face-to-face relationships with others. The illusion that we are the centre, with the ego as the master in the house, is an ideological story as powerful as the one that human beings are the centre of the world, set against the other sentient beings in the animal kingdom instead of living at one with them. These two ideological stories about us as being at the centre, the centre of being, are really only one evidenced, questioned and challenged by a radical psychoanalytic perspective. Psychoanalysis challenges the ego's power over us and over everything else.

Psychoanalysis, in its critique of the ego, poses each of us with a choice, as to whether we will continue to attempt to dominate ourselves and others and nature or find a different way of being with it. This choice is already liberating, but also revealing. It makes us discover at least three things about power: first, power is not inevitable, it is not something that must be either exerted or suffered; secondly, power cannot be exerted without being simultaneously suffered, as the domination of the other needs and presupposes the domination of oneself; thirdly, there is the same power involved in the ego that suffocates us, in what makes us oppress others and in what is destroying the world around us.

Psychoanalysis can help us to get out of our ego and to fight on the outside against the power that keeps us locked inside. The battlefield is outside, in the natural and sociocultural world, beyond the narrow conscious borders of our individuality. With the unconscious, then, we move from a conception of the ego separated from the world as an 'environment' to that of radical liberating ecology, of psychoanalytic ecosocialism. To do that, we must reclaim the world, and reclaim our power in the world.

Power

What is *power?* Power, as conceived of in psychoanalysis, is always there where the ego imposes itself, but it is never truly ours as individuals. Even when we believe we have power, it is not we who have it exactly and totally. Rather power is also what owns us and alienates us by exerting itself either through us or upon us, by dominating us to force us either to suffer or to exert domination, by exploiting us either as exploiters or as exploited, as masters or as lackeys, as consumers or as workers, as sellers of goods or as commodities. In all cases, by being possessed by power, we are alienated, we become alien to ourselves, and then we cease to be ourselves in order to become what power wants us to be.

Psychoanalysis offers us a vision of power as something decentred from the subject, something uncontrollable that is suffered even when exerted, something that always implies an alien and alienating unconscious substrate. This vision is necessary as a complement to most leftist views of power as something that is 'possessed', consciously exercised over others, wielded in such a way as to dominate people.

It is certainly true that there are those with power, the 1%, as well as rulers and macho leaders of many different private and state enterprises, those who enjoy their deliberate humiliation of those beneath them. But we need to take care, not to turn critical analysis of society into a gigantic conspiracy theory, and we know that conspiracy theories actually often function as poisonous injunctions that distract us from the real problem, from the patriarchal and colonial capitalist system, to target scapegoats, the case of antisemitic conspiracy theories being the most prevalent.

Marxism, and the many allied theories and practices of liberation from the feminist and anti-colonial movements are not conspiratorial delusions searching out those who exercise power, but systemic structural analyses of the ways that everyone is subjected to multiple intersecting regimes of power. These analyses coincide with what we learn from psychoanalysis. The view of power we present here is thus not only designed to complement those that energise liberation movements, but also to function as a resource for the critical analysis of false paths which actually, despite the best intentions of activists, depoliticize the struggle by individualizing, personalizing, and psychologizing politics.

The fundamental problem does not lie in certain individuals or in their actions, much less in their inclinations, their psychological profile or their personality traits. The fundamental problem is the structure that unconsciously makes them who they are and behave as they do. That structure is economic and symbolic, and so it is political, as profoundly political as the unconscious which operates with it and against it. Psychoanalytic politics that attends to the unconscious, to what is at the root, is therefore a more radical way of thinking about power. That which is unconscious to us in our social relationships and our personal experience has a powerful structuring effect on the way we understand the world and how we reproduce it or try to change it.

Psychoanalysis speaks of power and alienation endemic in a world that reduces human capacities and even human beings to the status of things to be bought and sold. We are pitted against others as we compete to sell ourselves by selling our knowledge, our ability, our life, our labour power. Our creative labour is then turned against us as something controlled and sold by our masters or by ourselves at the service of our masters, even doing our masters' work, controlling and selling labour, our labour.

Whether through other people, through things or through ourselves, our masters control us, make us do their bidding, which is sometimes also our own. We do what they do and what they do to us, even though they know not what they do, driven by the insatiable search for profit, driven into self-destructive attempts to dominate others. They alienate us and alienate themselves as they engage in the destruction of so many other lives, and in the devastation of the planet.

We are even charged with the task of carrying out the function of our masters, to imagine that we are little masters. This is what happens when we are given some authority as clients, owners, bosses, parents, husbands, teachers, evaluators, bureaucrats, policemen, soldiers, therapists, doctors, etc. This is small compensation and consolation. At least an insignificant part of all the power that is taken from us, of all the power that oppresses us, is returned to us. This can make us forget our oppression and exploitation. The pity is that forgetting it makes us all the more exploitable, makes us continue to be exploited, losing more than we gain. The little power we receive as individuals makes us collectively surrender ourselves to power. It works to lock us in place when we are told that it frees us.

Each one empowers themselves at the expense of ourselves. This is how something crucial for psychoanalysis happens: we separate each one of ourselves from our bodies and our relation to these bodies is perverted. We enslave our own bodies, we reify them, and we use them as means to fulfil the obligations or satisfy the ambitions of each one of us. This is what 'social models' of disability also teach us; that bodies are made to function in this world as ideologically 'complete' productive objects, and if they do not they are 'disabled'. The image of the complete self-sufficient body that is challenged by radical disability activists is as ideological as the image of the complete self-sufficient self that is challenged by radical mental health and 'anti-psychiatry' activists.

The ego of each one of us is constantly used to take over our bodies. We are spiritually exploited as individuals in order to materially exploit us as a collectivity. Social exploitation would be impossible without the complicity of an ego that is usually the weakest link in the community. This vulnerable point can be treated through psychoanalysis with the purpose of regaining collective power.

Our psychoanalytic view of power is of it as something we can seize collectively. We can take the power, and use it progressively to shape society and ourselves. We are not against power but against its imaginary reduction to the level of the individual, and we are for it as a creative force. We know that power can free us and serve us to create another world, better than this one, if we exercise it collectively, thus contradicting the dominant ideology that makes us imagine that power always belongs to the ego, as if individuals were the only subjects and were owners of their actions.

Common-sense views of society and of the nature of power operate ideologically, obscuring the root causes of alienation. We claim, in contrast, and in opposition to this ideological representation of society, that alienation plus power in this miserable world is the unconscious. In this sense, the unconscious is politics, and we must learn how to appreciate how our actions are unconsciously organised, all the better to act in a collective way against power, and to put an end to the most extreme destructive forms of alienation that are endemic under capitalism.

Rationality in the trap of the ego

Some forms of psychoanalysis, particularly those that have become mainstream and incorporated into adaptive institutions in the English-speaking world, see the ego as king, and aim to restore it to the throne in the clinic. The aim in adaptive conservative psychoanalysis is to make the ego the master in the house. In this way, the most radical proposals of Freud are betrayed, and the ego is assumed to be the seat of rationality.

This rationality is, of course, the kind of bourgeois individual rationality that is so beloved of ideology under capitalism, colonialism and patriarchy. This is rationality in the trap of the ego, and very different from the collective reason we together create in movements of resistance to power and movements of liberation. In order to connect with and create that collective reason we need to connect through the unconscious, to find ourselves there instead of losing ourselves in the ego.

The unconscious is everything of us that escapes individual reason, a sometimes necessary creative context which we cannot but inhabit, but an aspect of our humanity that is turned into a 'dark' force that is then viewed as a threat in bourgeois ideology. Negative images of what is dark, symbolic racism, often accompany such ideological images of the ideal self as master in the house, a heteropatriarchal illusion. This ideology, which is suspicious of both the unconscious and our body and collectivity, restricts us to the individual psychological sphere, the sphere of the conscious ego. Isolated in the ego, confused with it, we can forget the unconscious and dedicate ourselves to the subjugation of our own body.

The task of each of us is then to control our body and put it at the service of capitalism. This is why we subdue and master it, we treat it as a slave, as a machine that must labour for oneself and for others. We are then, in a personal drama that is becoming an ecological cataclysm, pitted against nature itself, nature viewed as a threat first inside of us, then outside of us. Our alienated state of being cuts us off from our own creative labour, suspicious of others, fearful of losing control of our own bodies and pre-emptively distrustful and destructive of nature as such.

Science

Total ecocide, the irreversible sacrifice of the world, begins with the immolation of our own body on the altar of the ego. This immolation is in turn the outcome of our alienation. Only by becoming something as the ego, something so alien to who we really are, can we destroy ourselves and destroy the entire world. In any case, there is no place left for the world when we totalize, under the total form of our ego, the individuality in which we are alienated. Our alienation is also an 'objectification'—including turning subjects and human relations into objects—and *science* is thereby transformed, distorted, from being a tool of practical analytic understanding into a tool of control.

We know the 'scientific' expressions of objectification in mainstream psychology. Instrumental 'science', which is an ideological form of scientific reason and which is based on a model of 'prediction and control', turns us into objects, an objectification of the subject which psychoanalysis speaks against. Once objectified, the subject transmutes into the ego. This ego is no longer the subject. It is something totally alien to the subject. It is something we get alienated into, lost in.

We are so alienated in the ego that we no longer see it as something alien. We become confused with the ego which in turn is confused with other egos. We can no longer distinguish ourselves from others, aiming to mimic others instead of recognising their value as something different to us. Then our relation to groups and communities is reduced to mimicry, to being like the others, instead of being different, instead of creative argumentative debate with them. In the process, political action is reduced to pure 'identification', mimicry that was the basis of the 'group psychology' that made the bourgeois-individualist Freud so fearful of the masses.

We have ended up reducing ourselves to an image of each one of us, separate, each one an isolated individual, locked inside the ego. We try in vain to recover ourselves through the ego, the ego that actually cuts us off from our world. So this world becomes alien to us, a product of alienation, a threatening 'dark' frightful unconscious instead of the wider ground of our being in the ensemble of social relations that makes us who we are and in collective struggle that may remake the world as a better place more respectful of the planet we inhabit.

The ego, in which we are all the more alienated at the very moment that we imagine that we are escaping the world and protecting ourselves, is thus, among other things, the crystallisation of bourgeois and colonial ideological commonsense. It is the model of humanity that has been imposed throughout the world through colonialism, imperialism and globalized capitalism. It is an allegedly civilized and implicitly white and masculine ego that speaks as if it guards the developed world from barbarism, but it is itself barbaric. It is presented as the only rational force, but its 'rationality' is profoundly irrational.

The kind of logic the ego perpetuates is that of instrumental science that aims to predict and control nature in order to subjugate and exploit it, always with the ultimate purpose of producing profits for capital. This enterprise, which is now implicated in the ecological devastation of our planet, underpins the discipline of medical psychiatry and psychology. It is at one with a peculiar pathology of normality, destructive stereotypical masculine rationality, a 'mental illness' of so-called normal man under capitalism and colonial rule. This is where we turn the metaphor of 'illness' around against those in power in the psy professions who so often use that metaphor against us.

In psychiatry instrumental rationality uses a disease model to treat our distress as if it were an illness, blind to the fact that it is present-day society that is 'sick'. It is this kind of rationality that also underpins scientific research, research that is dedicated only to pragmatic profitable private and capitalist state programmes of development, development which cares nothing for the singularity of each subject and is equally dismissive of creative labour. This kind of science accumulates knowledge as if it were capital, as if the 'facts' were commodities, often enclosed and traded as commercial items shrouded in secrecy. Little wonder that conspiratorial theories about the nature of power in the world thrive in this ideological context.

Psychoanalysis works upon the kind of subject who suffers at the hands of instrumental science. Our own psychoanalytic 'science' is very different. It is not instrumental but ecological, noticing the interconnection between things and our place in the world, the activist not as an object, but as a subject.

Ethics

The normal pathology inherent in the ego has also pen-
etrated the psychoanalytic field. A dominant ideological
reading of the clinical aim of psychoanalysis, a reading
inaugurated by Freud himself, is that 'where it was, there
ego shall be', as if the destructive illusory centre of bourgeois man must be fortified at the expense of the otherness
that lies in and around him, in and around us. This image
of the strengthening of the individual ego expresses the
most bourgeois aspect of psychoanalysis, and exposes a
key contradiction in Freud's own work.

This image of the strong ego that is compounded
by an image of the subjugation of nature was very much
of its time, and ecosocialist politics has done so much to
challenge it. Freud's statement about the aim of psychoanalysis entailing a strengthening of the ego against what
is 'it', other to it, against what is unconscious, continues
with the often-cited claim that this work is 'the work of
culture', something that Freud likens to 'the draining of
the Zuider Zee', the reclamation of territory in the The
Netherlands from the sea.

The bourgeois vision of psychoanalysis reduces it to an instrument in the typically modern combat of
the human ego against nature, against the 'it', against the
unconscious. Distancing ourselves from this reading, we
return to the ethical grounding of radical psychoanalysis
as a critical psychology in which we aim to be ourselves
where 'it' was, not to dislodge it, but to find the broader compass of radical progressive subjectivity there. It is
possible to reclaim and re-read that statement about the
aims of psychoanalysis, and to point out, for a start, that
the 'draining of the Zuider Zee' in the Netherlands of

Europe was actually a work of reclamation that enabled the people to live on that land. It was not at all a driving back of nature, but involved a new way of living on it, with it. Perhaps the same can be achieved through psychoanalytic work.

Let us reclaim psychoanalysis as a radical force, asserting that 'where it was, there we shall be'. We can exist as people with history, with our past and future, with interests and desires, with ideas and shared ideals, where there is now only unthinking repetitiveness and amnesia, demagogy and spectacle, robots and data, numbers and fatalities, things and relationships between things, commodities and exchange-value, capital and transactions.

Where capitalism works repetitively and automatically, there has to be our life, our truth, our thinking, our memory, a kind of radical 'repetition' that opens up something new rather than replicates it as the same as what it was before. We must remember and reflect, and act to free ourselves from the inertia of economy and ideology. This, just as the colonial masters must learn something about their place in the world and their history if any of them are to redeem themselves.

Psychoanalysis shows us that through a constructive progressive engagement with the unconscious, with what is unconscious to us, what 'we shall be', can be, but, and this is a crucially important lesson from anti-colonial struggle, we are not condemned to be the same in all historical and cultural contexts. We cannot say whether any particular aspect of our psychology is timelessly and universally true, including present-day theories about the unconscious.

Freud's work opened a path to an understanding of what is other to us, to the way we create and draw upon a hidden context, background, to our conscious action, but it needs to be constantly reworked if we are not to fall into the ideological trap of turning that 'unconscious' into a kind of container inside the head or a mystical realm with a religious message. What was discovered by Freud is not outside the world, but is situated in a culture and in a moment in history. Psychoanalysis needs to remain aware of its own culturally and historically specific character as diagnosis and treatment of present-day ills in the Western world.

Against a destructive ideology of scientific knowledge that arose in the West, and which was used as part of colonialism to segregate us and turn us into objects, we reclaim all that was positive about this historical development in such a way as to understand better how we are connected with others at a deep unconscious level. There is no 'collective unconscious' of the kind peddled by mystical Western writers who seek to compensate and complement what is done to us by their scientific reason, but there are opportunities for collective action where each of us find and activate what is unconscious to us in our relation to others. We must be sure that we are more and can do more than what is imagined by our individual consciousness trapped in certain forms of science and ideology.

What will liberate us is not esoteric mysticism, but neither will imperialist and generalizing scientific dogmatism. Against globalised Western 'science', we value what is singular about the human subject and what other civilizations and indigenous cultures have developed from their own resources. We know that we must break the mirror of the West and of our ego in order to reach the world and ourselves. Our future is beyond our present day patriarchal and colonial bourgeois individuality.

So, against the false alienated rationality of the individual ego, we put our bets on and our political energy into the construction of progressive collective alternatives that operate according to a different logic, that operate according to a logic of the unconscious, working with it, finding aspects of our subjectivity, our humanity in it. We do not idealise the unconscious, but we acknowledge its role in shaping who we are, just as we have already collectively shaped it in our cultural-political activity and then been silenced. What is not said, what cannot be thought is still present to us. It may be liberating, but it remains hidden, usually unacknowledged.

We pit ourselves against others in this wretched world instead of joining them in a collective struggle. We separate, we confront each other, we lose ourselves in what we are, but we are still here, among ourselves, in the unconscious. It is psychoanalysis that draws attention to that realm of human activity, a realm necessary to us as beings that speak, human beings that use language to communicate our hopes and fears to each other and weave together a critical analysis of the world, a world we reject, and images of another world we want to build.

Otherness, of psychoanalysis

The language we inhabit as human beings is the ground of our being, but as we speak and attempt to control the meaning of every word, we fail. Something always escapes, is beyond us, and in this miserable world this beyond is structured ideologically as an unconscious that is 'other' to us. This otherness is the unconscious dimension of our being that is always in a strange unbidden way present to us through its effects as the other side of the language that we speak.

Otherness is the realm of psychoanalysis. Although the psychoanalytic perspective opened up in Europe, Freud was both 'European' and set apart from that culture. Perhaps that is why he came to know something of the unconscious. A radical psychoanalytic perspective is inseparable from a culturally and historically determined estrangement from a certain kind of language which is also characterized by its cultural and historical specificity. Psychoanalysis, created at the margins of Western culture by Freud and his followers, most of whom were Jews subject to antisemitic exclusion, was itself 'other' to that culture, and so very well positioned to notice what was at the edges of bourgeois 'respectable' commonsensical consciousness, the consciousness of those with power.

Now there are other excluded and marginal dimensions of language. These dimensions are made visible by protests against capitalism, against patriarchy, against racism, against neocolonialism, against Islamophobia, against exclusion of disabled people, or against the devastation of the planet. It is the liberation movements that enable us to notice aspects of othering, visual images and symbolic representations of the unconscious that have been created in the context of globalisation, a globalisation through which psychoanalysis itself has spread around the world.

We notice, with the feminist movement, for example, the way that Freud referred to femininity as a 'dark continent', with the implication that there was some deep connection between this 'dark continent' of femininity and the unconscious. Then we are able to configure the task of psychoanalysis in the clinic and the task of political struggle in a new way that is feminist as well as being socialist.

As a political task, feminism poses men with a choice, whether they are to continue with their own macho individualist way of exercising power in line with a certain 'rationality', the rationality of the ego, or whether they will connect with the more intuitive collective and caring modes of being that are conventionally and stereotypically assigned to the position of women in patriarchal society. In other words, will we learn something from the so-called dark continent, as Freud did with the hysterics, or will we just continue to oppress and exploit the unknown and mysterious, as the West has done with the other cultures of the world?

The anti-colonial and anti-racist movements, meanwhile, aim to reclaim what is ideologically configured as a barbaric uncivilised 'dark continent', and this progressive political task also has deep implications for the way we re-read and transform psychoanalysis so that it might work alongside those movements in the clinic. Bourgeois rationality, and the mistaken aim of strengthening the ego, is a symptom of the unbearable whiteness of colonial reason.

This 'whiteness' of being was implicitly put in question by those, Jews, who first invented psychoanalysis, and now we connect with what is rendered unconscious to us in such a way as to make that critique of hegemonic whiteness explicit. We 'colour' in whiteness so it is no longer invisible to us, so that it no longer operates in such a way as to be a threatening unconscious inside us and around us.

Division

We cannot colour in whiteness or de-patriarchalize social relations if we are not aware of the complex way in which language operates and is structured. The first thing to know is that there is something in the nature of language, of our nature as speaking beings, which divides us, for we cannot say everything. This subjective *division* is unavoidable. We must bend to a symbolic system we cannot completely master when we speak, and so we become divided subjects, affected by something unconscious to us. Our division is inevitable. We must live with it. What is important is how we make sense of that division and what sense we give to it.

What we do know, and what psychoanalysis works with, is that the sense we make of our subjective division is filled with ideological content, as is the unconscious itself. Ideology mediates the experience of our divided condition. This condition, in which the unconscious functions as a place that speaks of our distress, is ideologically externalized, prolonged and exacerbated in particular alienating divisions of the subject, those that are characteristic of life under capitalism.

Each one of us is divided by the capitalist system and by its accompanying forms of rule. Patriarchy, for example, divides us between heterosexual male domination and those dominated, assimilated to denigrated femininity, and other kinds of sexuality. Likewise, colonialism divides us between apparently rational civilisation and the pathologising of so-called 'barbarians' who dare to resist it.

The ideological expressions of our subjective division in this alienated world are denounced and neutralized and transcended in the practice of the liberation movements. The anti-capitalists, the anti-colonialists, the anti-racists, the feminists, the lesbian, gay, transsexual, queer activists and others, many others, have fought and continue to fight effectively to free us from individualised power and instrumental science which reinforces a potent dominant image of what it is to be powerful. They open up a path, a psychoanalytic path to the unconscious, against powers that use our divided condition to dominate us by reinforcing an individual ego identified with colonial and patriarchal capitalism. Defying our ego, liberation movements can enable each of us to stop dominating ourselves, betraying ourselves. Betrayal and domination are things we can leave behind.

The unconscious is spoken into being by us when we interact with each other. It does not exist prior to our relational existence as speaking subjects. It needs us, all of us, and not just each one of us, to exist through what we say to each other, but also by virtue of this, and this is crucial to the progressive political role of psychoanalysis, the unconscious can connect us with collective action. It can thus help us to recover ourselves, to free us from what oppresses, represses and suppresses our collective existence, free association.

What we may never get free of is the division of the subject. We cannot say if this division can ever be healed, perhaps not, but the pain of that division can be alleviated. Relief may come from participation in liberation movements, from the challenge to ideology that is offered by psychoanalytic method in the clinic and by progressive reshaping of psychoanalysis that connects with explicit political action. We will say more in the following chapters about the method of 'free association' that taps into the unconscious such that the unconscious speaks back to us, so that we do not merely speak it into being.

So, we need psychoanalysis allied with and informed by collective struggle, a theory and practice that critically addresses the ideological representation of the subjective division which creates and perpetuates the unconscious as if it is only something inside us and threatening to us. The enemy is also outside and we must fight there against it. Alongside the clinical work is a political task of mobilising unconscious forces while analysing which forces perpetuate ideology and which tend to our freedom. We need to analyse and speak and act so that we make history instead of simply repeating it. *Repetition* next.

3

In an alienated world marked by exploitation and oppression, a world in which we must also be alienated from ourselves in order to contribute to our own exploitation and oppression, we live with alienation as something unconscious to us. We do not know the alien forces that govern us and put us incessantly in the same kind of situations. We only know that we are in the same predicament for the umpteenth time and that we cannot finally free ourselves from it. This is the character of *repetition*, a fundamental concept in clinical psychoanalysis where we can see people attempting to escape toxic and destructive relationships, imagining they are free and then repeating those patterns again with new partners.

We are subject to the repetitive nature of language, of familial and cultural and ideological words and phrases and narratives that keep telling the same stories about who we are and what it is impossible for us to achieve. Each attempt to change leads us down another path to the same place. And we are symbolically and bodily subject to the repetition of contradictory failed solutions to socially-structured material problems.

The fantasy that something different must happen then also obscures the underlying real nature of repetition and failure. We believe that we stop repeating when we change partners, when we learn from our experience or when we modify certain behaviour patterns, but in the end the same thing always happens.

Little wonder that such repetitive patterns of escape and unwitting unconscious reconstruction in new contexts of very old relationships should also haunt left organisations. These organizations also repeat toxic and destructive relationships, as well as situations of abuse, oppression, intolerance, violence, demotivation, boredom, heartbreak, and rupture. It may well be true that those who fail to learn from history will end up repeating it, but it seems that even that learning leads again and again into the same kinds of dead end.

We urgently need a psychoanalytic perspective on what histories of failure are doing to liberation movements who at some self-destructive level seem to enjoy suffering their repetitive defeats, how this compulsion to repeat manifests itself as something symptomatic in our political practice, and how we might have the freedom to know what it is we are repeating so we might avoid failing or at least fail better and actually learn from history.

Histories of failure

Capitalism, colonialism and patriarchy have a deep structure in common that concerns our subjectivity and our ability to deal with certain objective conditions we know are deeply destructive to us and to our comrades in struggle. It is as if our lives are driven by unknown and uncontrollable forces that make us find ourselves interminably in the same situations. It is as if these forces prevent us from transforming our lives and instead force us to repeat mistakes and defeats. The fact is that we do not stop repeating even what we do not want to repeat, and this is something the left knows only too well.

This is where the unconscious kicks into action, impelling us to make again the moves we surely know will end badly. Something in our historically-constructed nature decides, imposes itself upon and structures our histories of failure, and psychoanalysis shows us how these histories carry us along inside and outside the clinic.

Unconscious social structures, as with explicitly ideological messages that benefit those who enjoy power over us and commonsense explanations that mislead us about the nature of human action, effectively neutralize our efforts to subvert them. We need to ask why that is so and how that process works. The problem is that the same structures even absorb our efforts to understand them, and use them to their advantage. One way or another, they make us collude in reproducing what we intended to transform. The changes seem to occur only on the surface. What dominates us is recomposed and disguised with new masks. This would be bad enough if it operated only at the level of the capitalist state and in apparatuses of power that repeat sexist and racist oppression, but it is worse than that. Unconscious repetition means that this is not only being done to us. We also do it to ourselves.

New ways of organising too often end up leading us back to the same place we started from. This is not only a problem of the 'old left' who search in their textbooks for analysis of past situations and vainly try to make those analyses work in the present, but it also applies to new social movements who imagine that they have broken free from social structures but end up replicating those very structures they unconsciously know so well in new conditions.

In both cases it is as if we are in a labyrinth with no way out, in which we always decide on the same strategies, stay trapped inside the same closed field of tried and tested explanations; and then, logically, whatever we decide fails. We seem to change so that everything stays the same. Our great revolutionary gestures are nothing but small readjustments and rearrangements of the same. It seems so often that we only know how to innovate by finding new ways to repeat what there is instead of really creating something new out of the current conditions. Whatever we do, we always end up doing approximately the same. We do what we must do. We do not own our history. It seems to own us.

Enjoyment

This repetition is unconscious, and so it carries with it not only an uncannily familiar narrative that reassures us about who we are, but something else that is often difficult to acknowledge, *enjoyment*. Yes, it is true, we can see it around us in the stupid failed strategies of our comrades and in rival organisations, but it is more difficult to own up to it when we are caught up in this enjoyment. We enjoy not only saying triumphantly 'we told you so' when things turn out badly again, but also rejoicing in waiting for an already known outcome and shutting away the fear of something unpredictable happening.

It is not only bourgeois psychology that is obsessed with 'prediction and control'; we are also condemned to repeat the past precisely because we think we know what will happen in advance. The leap into an unknown future that is so crucial to the practice of the liberation movements is so many times sabotaged by them, and then there is a deadly collusion with power instead of an authentic challenge to it.

There is another aspect to this enjoyment that only psychoanalysis can effectively describe and work with, and help us find a way through, which is that this peculiar unconscious enjoyment is bound up with suffering. Of course we suffer in this miserable world. That is why we rebel and seek to change it. However, in addition to what unites us as humanity, something of that history of misery—personal and political misery that is intertwined in such a way as to chain us to where we came from—brings with it a kind of suffering that is recognisably ours.

A question haunts us from the unconscious as to what we would be if we had to live without it. That is what gives accusations against our political enemies and then self-recriminations such a potent poisonous sting. They point to who we are by placing us in the position of what we aspire to be. This position of our ideal allows us to enjoy our own suffering.

In the clinic that contradictory enjoyable suffering can be unravelled as it transforms itself in our speech from being a seemingly unresolvable contradiction into a symptom that is then structured dialectically in such a way as to enable us to find a way through it, to transcend it. In the political realm that intimate link between enjoyment and suffering is so much more effective, as an unconsciously structured knot of language and emotion, because there is no way to solve it, as there is, at present, no direct equivalent to the clinical work in political practice. Liberation movements often lack the means to manage their enjoyment of suffering, of repetition, so they can re-appropriate their history, own it for themselves and make it instead of suffering it.

Usually we do not make our own personal and political history, but we suffer it, often as if it was out of our control and out of our comprehension. We just let ourselves be carried away by inexorable determinations such as family dynamics configured by patriarchal power or as the destructive class structure defended by the capitalist state. In both cases, and in cases of racism and other forms of oppression, a combination of secrecy and ideological mystification results in an incomplete resolution of each of the problems that are thrown up, and thrown in front of us as obstacles.

Those difficulties and contradictions that are not solved are repeated, and as we live them we are thereby subject to repetition ourselves. We repeat what we do not solve in our lives. We do not solve it because we do not understand it, because we do not even know exactly what it is, because it is partly unknown to us, because it is partially forgotten, unconscious. As it cannot be remembered, it must be repeated.

Psychoanalysis teaches us that we repeat what we cannot remember because we find it intolerable, too humiliating, shameful, distressing, even horrifying and traumatic. What we do not even have the courage to remember is paradoxically what we have to repeat. Repeating is an unconscious way of remembering what is inadmissible to consciousness.

We repeat what we least want to repeat; our worst defeats, the abuses of which we were victims, the wounds that constituted us as what we are, the gestures by which we were conquered and subdued, our fall from grace, our colonization, the origin of our oppression and our exploitation. All this is repeated even when it is fought against. Our struggles fail to free us from the repetitive refrain of our history. This history is also the history of what we keep repeating.

Whether we like it or not and whether we like psychoanalysis or not, history itself is a repetitive process of attempts and failures to overthrow the existing order of things. We cannot stop repeating and succeed once and for all because we do not make history in conditions of our own choosing. We act in given conditions and according to different patterns of oppression that lock these exploitative alienating conditions of production and consumption into place. These patterns also fulfil a crucial function; to block the crucial necessary building of collective self-organisation.

Suffering

We are not permitted, not given the space, not authorized to organize ourselves because such self-organization would produce something new. The prohibition of novelty is a powerful message that is sent to us consciously, but also on the unconscious level, where it is more difficult to notice and so more difficult to refuse. That is how there is *suffering* when we obey the demand to enjoy. The message prescribes that everything has to continue functioning as usual. Our enjoyment and suffering are tied together in the idea that we must continue to be organized by the capitalist system to fulfil its ends—its own and not ours—and that only in that way can we be happy, and we then ask ourselves why we are not happy.

When we break from this logic, refuse to allow the capitalist system to take precedence over our own desires, there is a powerful message that then repeats this logic, a message that tells us that the correct thing is to accept the rules of the game, that we have received a lot from the system, that things could be worse, that we should not rebel because we will endanger our family and friends and comrades, that we should feel guilty for every partial success as well as every failure.

At the one moment, it feels as if this struggle will never end, that the world will never change, and at the next it feels as if the ends are always the same. They impose a repetitive, destructive and self-destructive logic of labour and consumption, of more and more labour and consumption, but also of the most diverse routines of exploitation and oppression. In this way, class power, racism and sexism and other discriminatory ideological practices must repeat their function of enabling the accumulation of material resources, of the realisation of profit and the concentration of wealth among those deemed fittest to embody and represent the needs of capital.

So, instead of treating each failure as yet another surprise, yet another grim reminder that our hopes to change the world must be confined to the realm of fantasy instead of reality, we need to understand a deeper and more dangerous aspect of our unconscious lives. We repeat because we learn to repeat, because we do not know how to act otherwise, and not because it is an 'instinctive' behaviour. No instinct makes us enjoy suffering. Failure is not hard-wired into us as biological organisms, but embedded in our history as speaking beings, a history that is structured around dimensions of class, race and gender, a history of domination that is also often unfortunately repeated in the very organisations that we have built to overthrow this wretched system.

Our liberation movements repeat what we live in the family. In the psychoanalytic clinic we can see how the intimate link between suffering and enjoyment is forged in our family history as a function of our sexuality. Later, in political organisations, that intimate link is played out in more overt battles over status and power. The question is how to break from that collusion with forms of social relationship we know are wrong, and open up spaces for reflection and action. It is possible to trace a path in a more progressive direction by turning the compulsion to repeat into that which psychoanalysis conceptualises as the force that drives the symptom.

Compulsion and symptom

The repetition of failure and structure has an understandable and recognisable aspect. We know well, for example, how tempting it is for workers' representatives to succumb, to savour the crumbs of enjoyment that are offered to them by employers. Time away from work can be offered to them during which they fraternise with the bosses, perhaps even sharing drinks and meals around meetings, and this draws them into a lifestyle which provides comforts they do not have when living among their comrades in the factories or the fields.

Workers can be seduced by their bosses to the point of wanting what the bosses want, even eventually wanting the bosses to win, obviously at the expense of the workers. This is how workers can seek their own failure by alienating their desire in the desire of the other, by adopting the other's discourse, the enemy's point of view. The most serious consequence in the long-term is that bourgeois structures begin to embed themselves in a layer of the workers' movement, and the values of the employers, including the fiction of 'shared interests' and the 'common good', take hold.

We can see then a material basis for the well-known Marxist argument that ideology operates through the spread among the working population of the worldview of the employers; here it is indeed the case that the ruling ideas are the ideas of the ruling class. Here there is a replication of ideology and structure, repetition of it at a sometimes conscious but more often an unconscious level.

Replication

Trades union representatives have privileges which can lead them to defend their particular interests as a bureaucratic layer within the workers' movement. Again, there is a *replication* of ideology and structure, and then demands for accountability and rotation of positions become important to combat this. However, even with these measures, it is very difficult to avoid certain effects of the structural determination of power positions. Colonialism also functions in exactly this kind of way, and this is why it somehow makes sense to speak of the workers' movement being 'colonised' by ruling class values and ideology.

In the case of colonialism, we see local representatives bought off by the invaders, and eventually they constitute a particular class layer that has more in common with the colonial masters than they do with the slaves they once were. We know well the phenomenon of colonial subjects returning to their countries and dressing and eating like their masters, differentiating themselves from the local population. With that enjoyment, however, comes suffering, and we also know that the colonial subject is torn between their loyalty to their people and to their masters, divided, anguished by the collusion they are invited into.

The subject is usually divided between replicating and not replicating the dominant economic structure and ideology. However, there is something more beyond this replication which a psychoanalytic approach to enjoyment and suffering draws attention to. Repetition is not the result of conscious choice, though of course there are times of crisis when the subject decides where their loyalty lies.

Those times of crisis are so anguishing precisely because something has to be grasped concerning this repetition, which is usually unconscious, uncontrolled and compulsive. Repetition compulsion materialises itself in the clinic in the form of the symptom, a particular symptom that the subject carries with them as an expression of conflict and pain. This psychic pain has a material basis which is a strange unconscious combination of personal life history and the history of the society in which people are told how they must enjoy and how they may suffer.

There is thus a two-fold repetitive process in everyday life under contemporary capitalism. The first aspect is usually understood as operating in the 'outer world', through the repetition of diverse forms of oppression and exploitation in social and institutional relations. Psychoanalysis has something valuable to say about this process because material political-economic forces also drag individuals into self-destructive patterns of behaviour.

These forces hook and reward individuals for behaviour that reproduces material structures of domination, of class and geopolitical power, as well as those of the family and the distribution of power between the sexes, and between the able-bodied and the 'disabled'. Sometimes there are symptomatic contradictions between those who resist dominant structures, with a resistance that speaks of freedom, and structural reactions characterized by their violence, by their violent repetition of protest that speaks of oppression.

The second aspect of this repetitive process operates ideologically, intimately bound up with the political-economic material structural domain but also intimately connected with the personal life-worlds of those subject to power, the so-called 'inner world'. This is the world we take refuge in, as if we could escape oppression inside ourselves, but we cannot, there is no escape into the individual self. As they speak of their experience of this process, subjects are prevented from speaking, their own standpoint is delegitimized and their accounts are systematically distorted.

The contradictions that emerge here are also symptomatic; that is, a conflict opens up between a repetition of complaint followed by failure that speaks of oppression and the kind of desire that speaks of freedom. The psychoanalytic clinical task is thus to

enable subjects to speak, to say something about their experience and their desire, and here, of course, the clinic becomes political, or rather it reveals itself as what it
always is, because the personal is, as socialist-feminism
proclaimed, political, or as we say in psychoanalysis, the
unconscious is politics.

Forgetting the unconscious makes us forget politics. This can happen when ideological or economic repetition accustoms us to what is repeated, petrifies and
naturalizes it, makes it appear as something inevitable,
as a necessary effect of the force of things or of human
nature. Psychology and other sciences intervene here to
offer us conceptions of humanity with which what is repeated is justified, rationalizing it, universalizing it and
depoliticizing it. We then forget politics because we forget that repetition is historical and can be interrupted
by those subject to it, by us, subjects. Psychoanalysis reminds us that these subjects exist, gives them the floor, lis-
tens to what they have to say about their symptoms and
thus should help us to re-politicize what is repeated and
manifested symptomatically.

It is when repetition becomes compulsive, the
repetition compulsion at the level of the subject that psychoanalysis treats in the clinic, that it can be condensed
into a symptom. Remember that the symptom is, at root, a
conflict, but a conflict of a quite particular kind. It is a conflict in which a desire or wish comes up against a prohibition, repression. The conflict between what is desired and
the forces that bear down on it, shutting out, repressing it,
is more complicated than it seems, and the complication
that psychoanalysis introduces into the picture also has
profound implications for how we conceptualise political
struggle. In progressive political struggle a desire for
freedom, and for much more, for a world in which we

will all be free, comes up against the forms of power that capitalism, colonialism and patriarchy mobilises against us. That is, desire comes up against repression.

We need to take care, however, to treat progressively emerging desires for change as historically created, not as expressing already-existing universal forces that spring as if from inside each individual subject or from human groups. Desire for freedom under these miserable conditions in the twenty-first century is very different from such desire at other points in history. Yes, of course, there is something in the human being that is creative and then distorted and held down by those with power, and, yes, that has most likely always been so.

The kinds of desires that we are aiming to act with now against contemporary systems of domination are created by us, historically created by us as historical beings; these desires are now articulated around an image of another world where there will be collective management of resources, an end to racist segregation, empowerment of women, inclusion of bodies of different kinds and the preservation of the planet. The demands we make are responses to what is denied us in this world now.

There is, of course, a popularised image of psychoanalysis that treats each individual as like a pressure cooker with instinctual forces pushing for release. That image is convenient for those who wish to reduce our struggle to a kind of resentment at natural civilised rules of behaviour in a society that has to balance the needs of each against the needs of the many. The point that our psychoanalysis makes about the conflict between desire and repression, however, is actually very different. It is the form of repression that itself gives rise to forms of desire. It is precisely what is prohibited that is called into being, incited, provoked, and then that prohibited desire can be articulated in reactionary or progressive ways, in self-destructive or creative ways.

A forbidden desire may seek to be satisfied in a subversive way that defies the various repressive devices that lock society into place, but it may also seek an adaptive, lucrative, exploitable satisfaction in capitalism, which involves repression, which is intrinsically repressive. The two expressions of the same desire can be opposed to each other in the individual sphere, but also in the social sphere. There are glaring contradictions between the perspectives of drug trafficking and the drug legalization movement, pornography and sexual liberation, fundamentalism and anti-colonialism, black capitalism and anti-capitalist anti-racism, eco-capitalism and true ecology.

In all cases, a truth is contradicted by its repressed and repressive, mystified and recovered expression. It is the same process as that which occurs in each individual existence where desire cannot avoid facing its recovery and justification by repressive devices. As it is with the individual in the clinic struggling to make sense of repression and struggling to make decided choices about what they want, so it is in the political realm as we collectively debate and create forms of organisation that will operate in a way very different from the forms of repression that attempt to manipulate our desires, exploit them and prevent us from speaking and acting.

Contradiction

These conflicts are condensed into a symptom when the clinical context enables the subject to transform the seemingly irresolvable conflict into a *contradiction*, and then this symptom can be treated dialectically. From existing fixed conditions of possibility for action, new possibilities are created. This is a clinical task that is also a political task, for it necessitates connecting the subject's life experiences with a critical reflexive dialectical understanding of the networks of relationships that have made them who they are.

If conventional psychology and psychologized psychoanalysis tend to seem apolitical, it is because their politics is generally geared to what is dominant and repetitive. That is not a genuine alternative because it is not distinguished from existing conditions of possibility which set restrictions on action and impose certain prohibitions in place. The singularity of the subject is a political matter, enabling us to speak against the conventional conservative psy professions that currently dominate us and cover over, obscure any radical alternative. This is because the psy professions tend to stamp their own orientation and coloration onto almost everything and because their own theories of the benefits of adaptation are repeated incessantly through almost everything that is done to us in this world.

That kind of adaptive politics is imposed on the subject when the psychologist speaks in their assigned place and reinterprets the life of their 'clients' based on what they, the professional, know and what we already know, that which is repeated incessantly, about what is psychologically normal and so socially normative. It is almost enough in the clinic to let the subject speak and to know how to listen with attention and patience—that which should be done in psychoanalysis—to end up discovering another politics, that of the subject's desire and their experience of repetition. Here the space of the psychoanalytic clinic is a space that operates in stark contrast to the repetitive functioning of the capitalist system. It does not correspond to that system's norms or standards of predictability, of adaptability and apparent flexibility.

The subject acts 'normally' by behaving in a predictable way, by being as repetitively assertive, possessive and competitive as they must be, by saying, thinking and feeling only what they should, by silencing their desire and experience, and by contributing, through their work and consumption, to a repetition and replication of the oppressive and exploitative material operations of capitalism. They are allowed, even encouraged to be flexible within the limits set for them in categories of identity, lifestyle and class position that can be harvested and sold back to them as 'market niches'.

These ideological and socioeconomic repetitions are inseparable and support each other. Its increasingly inextricable knotting represents one of the greatest strengths of the current neoliberal capitalist system and one of the greatest challenges for those who fight against it.

Tying together the material and the ideological, the structural and the symbolic aspects of rule and resistance, is the underlying and overarching problem we face today—the intrinsic complexity of global capitalism—and incomplete and distorted solutions available to us in the left and liberation organisations. At least we can clearly see the two forces in combat, both caught in repetition. On the one side, on the side of power, is the compulsive drive to accumulate and protect capital, fruit of exploitation, which takes on an obsessional and repetitive character. On the other side, on the side of resistance, are the organisations of the left that are too-often repetitively stuck in their own failed history, making the same mistakes.

The history of class struggles and the broader more fundamental process of liberation from different forms of oppression is one of repetition and failure, and also, remember, sometimes fortunate and often tragic chance events that are completely out of our control. This is the interminable, almost unendurable repetitive context which is then replicated inside the lives of individuals. Individuals are encouraged to imagine that they are free and independent of this double material and ideological historical process so they feel this failure all the more deeply. They cannot bear the evidence that they have so little power over their lives. Nor do they know how they should deal with repetition and with its iron law, with necessity and with chance, with fatality and with destiny. Psychoanalysis works upon all this complex material and symbolic material.

In psychoanalysis, individuals speak, attempt to 'free associate', to say everything that comes to mind, and say it freely, without censorship. They seek to say something new, something unknown, but fail. As they fail, they hear themselves reiterate the same old stories, those they have been told about themselves, those that have materialized in their own lives. These stories must be repeated to prevent other stories from being told or occurring. Free association reveals to the subject the points in their speech where they cannot say everything, and, more significantly, where there are points of blockage, obstacles to speech and action. What begins to emerge at those points is another face of repetition, the recurrence of conflict, a conflict that contains within it both desire and repression.

So, the compulsion to repeat is unmasked and condensed in a symptom that can be transformed into a dialectically-organised contradiction at the heart of the subject's being, opening up new paths, the creation of new conditions of possibility for their speech and action. This psychoanalytic work in the clinic is not by any means a perfect model for political struggle, and we are not suggesting that it should function as any such model, but it offers powerful lessons for those who are struggling against power outside the clinic. In this way the strange limited freedom that appears inside the psychoanalytic clinic connects with the unpredictable forms of collective freedom that the liberation movements aim to create in the world.

Freedom to repeat, and fail better

A progressive lesson of psychoanalysis is that, against the compulsion to repeat, it is possible to open up new possibilities in which we may well continue being subject to repetition, for we cannot wish away the existence of the unconscious, but we can make more choices. We may not always succeed in getting what we want. Remember, we are *divided subjects*. Surely we will not even have absolute certainty that it is really us who want what we want. That would be impossible, at least in present-day society and for some time to come, because even if we were to free ourselves from the greatest social obstacles to our satisfaction, we would continue to be haunted by the history of domination and alienation that has shaped who we are and how we speak of ourselves. However, even if we continue to fail, we can achieve some real successes and make choices in such a way as to know better what the difference is between success and failure.

This is a space of freedom, a space opened up in a very limited way inside the psychoanalytic clinic, a space that we can open up even more in the political realm. This space should not necessarily exclude what is repeated. So far we have emphasised the restrictive limited aspect of repetition, repetition of the same, but we now want to draw attention to another aspect of repetition that always contains within it something different. The space of freedom that lies hidden inside repetition, and so often chained in the prison of the individual self by repetition compulsion, is a different space. It is a space of more and more tension, of increasing aggravation of contradictions, but also, for the same reason, of resistance, insistence and perseverance, and of unavoidable forms of displacement or symbolic distance with respect to what is repeated. It is not repetition of the same, but repetition that creates difference.

What is different also derives from repetition. What is repeated twice cannot be the second time the same as the first, precisely because it happens for the second time, because there has already been a first time, because it is already something repeated and not something new. Contexts change the meaning of different elements, life moves on, and repetition is then not merely the same but something also subtly, sometimes dramatically, different. This is a complex dialectical process, in clinical treatment and in politics.

Repetition can imply insistence or emphasis, but this repetition also gives itself away, reveals it, and so makes it annoying and unavoidable, even unbearable and unsustainable. All of this provokes different feelings, thoughts and behaviours regarding what is repeated. And if it continues to repeat itself, it can make the subject turn away from it, critically judge it from a distance, especially if the repetition takes place in a reflexive framework, such as that of psychoanalysis and liberation movements.

Signifiers

People repeat with their words the same things they have been repeating over and over again in their lives. Yes, that is true. Such is how they try to make sense of the way that material and ideological conditions of life are embedded in the unconscious and in their unconsciously-driven repetitive responses to events around them. At the very same time, as the blockages in their speech reappear again and again, they also repeat and experience those relationships of obedience that prevented them speaking out.

The difference is that now, in their own psychoanalytic process, they have another chance in the clinic for them to perhaps say what they did not say previously. When this happens, their words, as *signifiers*, enable and encourage them to move on and to take some distance from their old lives. Here there is limited and potential freedom.

Even when people repeat, their repetition is not simple replication of the same words, phrases and meaningful action, of the same symbolic elements of our oral, written or existential discourse that we conceptualise as 'signifiers'. Every signifier, every word or action or thing in the human world, is already part of a system of meaning that gives our signifiers value, make them understandable enough to people to function in the medium of communication and in ideology. These are the signifiers that make up the symbolic world we share in our different languages, the building blocks of that symbolic world.

The signifiers, with their repetitions and their connections, are heard by the 'analysand' who participates in a clinical experience of psychoanalysis. This 'analysand' is very different from the 'patient' treated by psychiatrists or the 'client' treated by psychologists. Our psychoanalytic analysand does the analysing. We analysts do not hand them a treatment; they take the cure into their own hands. They are subjects not objects. What they say is not interpreted by the analyst, but by themselves. Their interpretation of their words is done with more words that are added to the previous ones and that in turn must be interpreted by them. The most intimate meaning of these words is in themselves, in the complex relationships between them, and not beyond them, not in a mysterious depth that could only be divined by the analyst reading the symptom as if they were some kind of soothsayer or prophet.

We do not need to delve down beneath the surface to be able to work out how signifiers that operate in a system of meaning that is always beyond our control, unconscious to us, are operating. Signifiers operate according to what we dowith them, according to what they do with us, and they are always here, in what we say and hear. The term 'liberation', for example, is a signifier, and each political term we use to define who we are and what our collective identity can be is also a signifier, whether that is as 'worker', 'woman' or 'disabled' or 'indigenous'.

Signifiers are defined for us in a symbolic system, but we can take the initiative to rework them, rework their meaning. As happens at a collective political level, so in the clinic an analysand hears the signifiers that have been given to them by powerful others in their lives to define their identity, and seizes control, even for an instant, to remake them.

Signifiers take on different meaning according to their place in the contradictory ever-mutating language that we speak, the language that surrounds us and which we act upon when we change ourselves and when we change the world. We know this well from the attempts to reclaim signifiers that have been used to speak of us in an oppressive or repressive way, such as 'black' or 'mad' or 'gay'. We take these signifiers and own them again in our progressive political struggle, and say them with pride instead of shame.

The same things, actions and words, are never exactly the same, being situated in ever-changing contradictory cultural and historical contexts. At the same time, particular signifiers are charged with meaning for each singular subject, and 'liberation' may mean something different in different contexts. Psychoanalysis in the clinic attends to the specific role that signifiers play in someone's life. We may imagine that we know what they mean, but psychoanalysis shows us that we have to listen to signifiers with greater attention to reconstruct how they operate in a shared and individual symbolic system.

Our history, whether collective-political or personal-political, is not a fixed and rigid grid but is always open, depending on our struggle to make sense of who we are and the world we want to make. Our being and our aspirations contradict what is repeated, which, in turn, also contradicts itself. These contradictions, in a process of dialectical movement, cause instability of the system, either in the way of 'shock capitalism' that uses crises to reconfigure and strengthen itself or to give us space for freedom. It is up to us, to how we reflect and act, and whether we act collectively.

The repetition of the same is perpetuated by ideological lines of force and political-economic structures, force and structures that we resist because they place limits on our speech and action. Psychoanalysis can help us here to resist by giving us a space to experience and express how we repeat what we say about ourselves, and how we repeat what we do to perpetuate self-destructive patterns of behaviour. This space is effective insofar as it allows us to reflect on repetition instead of just repeating the same old familiar patterns of action.

So, in place of the repetition of the same, the clinic opens the space for something different to emerge; the absolute difference that makes a signifier as such, and a very different absolutely singular sense of our own subjectivity. This emergence of absolute difference is a victory that can pay the price of innumerable failures, and redeem them. We are condemned to repeat, but we are also driven to make a difference. We psychoanalysts can make a difference in the clinic by opening up a space for difference, a space for the subject to be different from what the rules of ideological common sense and its psychology manuals establish.

Likewise, liberation movements can make a difference in the world by differentiating themselves from the dominant ideology, by wanting to create a totally different world, by building a world in which difference is valued as a condition for being human. Repetition of failure is thus transformed into something different. Something in us drives us to do that, which is what we turn to next, in the next chapter, *drive*.

4

DRIVE: BODY, CULTURE AND DESIRE

Something compels us to rebel. When we are impelled to act it is as if we are a force of nature, and all the more so when we will make a difference. Indeed, in these moments, we can somehow be a force of nature; we can be with nature on this earth instead of colluding with the devastating capitalist logic which aims to subdue and exploit it, this is *drive*.

When we behave in a way adapted to the capitalist environment, our behaviour is not only destructive, but also has a false, artificial and superficial aspect. Instead, our impetus to rebel seems to come from the inscrutable depths of our body, from an animal part of ourselves that palpitates, surges forth beyond language. In reality, this impetus is intermeshed with speech, with an accounting for what we are doing and so also with who we are through words.

Language is inseparable from our body, from our most secret and transgressive impulses, which always have crucial elements already repressed. Repression, remember, does not merely press down on us but regulates speech and action in such a way as to create and structure our desire. If we do not understand that lesson from psychoanalysis we will still be trapped in what we are told we want instead of making collective choices about the kind of freer world we can construct for ourselves.

Words, entangled with our being, not only oppress, imprison, chain and immobilize us. They can also encourage us to act in order to free us from our chains. The resulting act can then be explained by an effective, subversive, revolutionary and perhaps liberating word. It will be a word, perhaps just 'no', or words, perhaps 'no, this is enough', intimately connected with action, with the body. What we are as human beings is grounded in our body as real, and shaped by language, by the symbolic system of culture, through which we desire others, and desire other bodies.

The drive springs forth at the border between the body and culture. This border, this edge is an injured, mutilated, extremely sensitive place, characterized by pain, shame, imbalance and impossibility. It is here where the drives emerge with their dynamic force that makes desire possible. These drives are the subject of this chapter, in which we speak of the nature of the body, its life and death, of the place of the drive, including for sex, in culture, and of our desire which is intimately connected to the desire of others.

Bodies, of life and death

We live in our bodies, but we are alienated from them. This alienation is intensified under capitalism when we fear for our lives if our body lets go of us, if it cannot function as labour power that we sell to others, if it cannot take us to work. Even though we live in our bodies, there is something strange about them, and it is when they cease to function that we experience them as something real, uncanny, unknown.

We can never know our body directly. Our understanding of our body is structured by the images we use to picture it to ourselves and the language we use to describe it to others. The body is mediated culturally by ideological misrepresentations. What we know of ourselves through ideology includes strange alienating ideas about our bodies, our bodies turned into objects to be bought and sold and consumed and enjoyed by others.

However, despite ideology and through combating ideology, we can also learn something more about our bodies as sites of refusal. We can then know something of our bodies that is very different from ideological misrepresentation of them, and then, when we speak with our body rather than against it we can find a way to speak the truth. This is something that psychoanalysis cues us into, the peculiar contradictory connection between bodies and words, our material being and signifiers.

Life

Signifiers elaborated through speech in psychoanalysis take the form of words with powerful effects, as powerful as the signifiers that tell us what our place in the world is, in the dominant ideological messages that structure this world. The word can be healing; it can heal psychic pain that has effects on the body, because it can be true and thus dispel the lies and silences that make us sick.

This is one reason psychoanalysis was called, by one of the first analysands, a 'talking cure'. The prohibitions, amnesia and ideological mystifications of patriarchal and colonial capitalism, such as those of our family and those of our own ego, can be neutralized, transcended by what we say. We speak the truth, and in the personal-political realm, we speak truth to power. It involves others, life.

There are true statements that concern not only me. Others suffer like me the effects of power that tries to divide us in order to defeat us one by one. Each of us has been locked in to our individual selves and suffers some form of oppression and exploitation. The silences and lies of ideology deceive us, confuse us and mislead us all. It is logical then that we feel impelled to look for each other and meet to speak and act, to denounce injustice and to rebel, to discover the truth and fight against power. Here again, for good or ill, we are in the realm of the drive.

This is life, this 'life drive', drive to speak and act. It is productive and collective, relational, and sexual. It is not locked inside us, but it exceeds us and overflows us; it is between us and outside of us; it makes us bond with others and thus weave the world around us. Everything that is of the subject, we psychoanalysts say, goes through the 'Other', through the otherness that is the mark of human subjectivity.

It is in the other and through the other that our drive makes us live. But something of this drive which takes us beyond ourselves, which is unconscious, beyond our conscious control, can also take on a mechanistic quality in which we feel driven. That is when what drives us turns into something inert, deadly, destructive and self-destructive. The drive then manifests itself as something more deadly, as a 'death drive'.

Every drive is potentially a death drive. Its deadly aspect prevails when we surrender to it, when we drop under its weight, when we get carried away by its inertia. Those are the times we unconsciously repeat the same actions and signifiers. Then we are subject to repetition, compulsion to repeat, subject to an automatic and destructive force, today embodied in the capitalist system.

Capital, conceived as a process, is pure satisfaction of the death drive, conversion of life into death, consumption of the living existence of workers and of nature to produce more and more money, dead money. However, at the same time, capital works and somehow lives with the vital energy of the workers, with their life drive that is still what is present to us, even when it transmutes into the death drive of the drive for profit, capitalism. The destructive and productive aspects of drive usually appear empirically united, indiscernible from each other, and can only be distinguished through radical theories of subjectivity and politics; theories such as Marxism and feminism and post-colonial and queer theory, and psychoanalysis.

Here we need historically-attuned psychoanalysis, psychoanalysis conceptualised as constituted historically, if we are to grasp the two-fold nature of drive as manifested in each historical period. In every moment drive is productive, creative, constructive, life, what it is within us enabling us to build links with others, to build culture and forms of political organisation, and to speak of other possible worlds. However, also at every moment, drive is also destructive and repetitive, death, that which is turned against ourselves and against those social links that sustain us, against nature and against culture.

The drive is what achieves satisfaction in the capitalist process that devours the planet and corrodes the various diverse human civilizations we have created. It is also, at the same time, what is impelling us to resist this widespread devastation and moving those who fight for their cultures, for the planet, for life and against capitalism. We must choose. This is the choice we face at every moment, and especially now. Our body can be at one with us when we act, but then our nature can be turned into a machine; then our alienated body is a machine turned against us.

Death

Capitalism has always done whatever it takes to strip us of our bodies. It has made them function as if independently of us through an ever-increasing division of labour. It has sharply divided us from them; it has made us despise and repudiate them; it has taught us to discipline and exploit them; it has set us against them. The fate of our bodies is the same as our lives. The capitalist system appropriates everything that lives in us to transform it into labour power and thus produce more and more capital, *drive*.

Today, in late stage capitalism in the twenty-first century, it is worse. It is as if the machines that we have created to relieve us from work have turned us into their slaves, and the imperative to make profit creates extra work, so we have less time instead of more. The possibilities that technology opens up are betrayed by the drive for profit, a drive that intensifies our exploitation and oppression. This imperative to make profit speeds

up production processes, and that acceleration of life under capitalism means that even more than ever our own
bodies are experienced as things alienated from us.

Under capitalism in the nineteenth century the
development of industry proceeded so fast and it did it
so destructively for nature and for culture, and with so
little care for the lives of workers, that it was as if everything that was solid melted into air. Now, with industrial
and technological development that are in the hands of
private companies or state enterprises that work on be-
half of capital, there is an alienating acceleration of this
process such that all that is left to us are the bodies we
inhabit, bodies that must work, bodies faced with ruin. It
is true that our bodies are alienated, but we can recover
them, at least in part, at least for moments. We need them.
It is only with them interwoven with speech, with true
speech, that we can act.

We are faced with a task which works at a contradiction. On the one hand there is the deadly deathly face
of drive. There are social structures in place that are dedicated to their own self-maintenance, structures person-
ified by those who benefit from them to hold onto their
power, to employ workers at the lowest possible wages
and to make the maximum amount of profit. This 'surplus value', that which those in power extracts from the
workforce, is drawn from our labour power, but this power is that of our life, that of our love and our creativity,
and so those with money and power pervert, instrumen-
talise, what drives us all to care for our loved ones and
have a creative impact in the world.

Our possible human community is replaced by
the capitalist, patriarchal and colonial system. Our tru-
est relations are subordinated to the relations of production, relations of exploitation that are shored up by other

relations of power, of men over women, and of racism and exclusion of those who are deemed not productive.

On the other hand, there is a drive for life, the loving face of the drive. There are the creative forces that are provoked and unleashed by capitalism, possibilities for innovation and development of culture. Within the very belly of capitalism are born the forces that will overthrow it, the collective forces that are gathered together in order for us to work creatively, and that allow us to learn from each other the value of working with each other rather than against each other.

These are the forces of production, the productive forces that also provide the energy of the liberation movements. The question is, whether we continue to let our masters and rulers determine how we will work and how we will enjoy and how we will service their own enjoyment, or whether we will take control and whether it will be us who will decide on our lives.

This is the drive today, a drive that runs through us and energises our bodies in an unconscious dynamic that is out of our control, a drive for innovation that is also channelled into a drive for profit. The drive is a bodily force that is the well-spring of life, of love and creativity, but has been turned against us so we not only feel subjected to it, but captured by its logic. Life and our nature, and nature as such are then experienced as threatening and frightening, and so we often separate ourselves from each other and close in on ourselves to try to escape.

Capital accumulates and gives life to the 1% while for the rest of us, those who work, those who sell their labour, and those who labour in the home to support those who must sell their labour, the drive is deathly. The drive is a death drive for the vast majority of those who live in capitalism. It is our historical development of this form of political-economy that makes it that the aim of life is death.

Culture, of sex, and more

One of the places where we experience our bodies taking us beyond ourselves, beyond our conscious control is in sex, and this sex which is so necessary to the reproduction of species, including the human species, also, for human beings takes on an unnecessary pleasurable, and sometimes painful, character. What drives us to sex is not at all necessary, and there are many who do without it, but this unnecessary enjoyment in sex poses a question about the nature of the body and its relation to enjoyment and suffering that drove the development of psychoanalysis.

It is often said that psychoanalysis is obsessed with sex, but it is more the case that psychoanalysis helps us to understand how it is that we feel driven to sex in a culture that is itself obsessed with a certain intensely ideological series of images of what sex is. This is the culture that demands that we work, and that prohibits forms of enjoyment that are not functional either to the reproduction and maintenance of the work-force through the family or for the realization of the surplus-value through consumption or for the cosmetic embellishment of capitalism through ideology. Although sex can thus be exploited, more is prohibited of sex in this culture than is demanded of it, and that prohibition itself has the bizarre uncanny effect of also inciting, provoking and demanding of us that we enjoy.

Prohibition

There is no sexual bodily activity for us human beings without *prohibition*, prohibition and transgression. Sex has become one of the key points at which we are driven by the hidden unconscious demand to transgress, and to enjoy transgressing in such a way that it is as if there is something deep inside us that must find release. It is then not surprising that the very sexual activity that should, we are told, bring pleasure, also often brings shame, guilt, loneliness, jealousy, violence, anguish, pain.

Sex has been so important to psychoanalysis precisely because it is a place where we see enjoyment and suffering so closely linked together. An alienated unhappy life links them together all the more closely, whether in reality as we experience sex or in fantasies about what we are missing, what we are told we are missing.

It is impossible to understand our current experience of sexuality without a conception of the unconscious, that which is beyond us and takes us beyond the ego, and of repetitive activity that gives us enjoyment and then also suffering, and of the drive; the drive gives life, and is an expression of life when sex operates, among other things, as the wellspring of reproduction. We are told that it should operate like that in this culture, but it does not. There is always more to it than we are told, more that is prohibited and incited, pushed out of consciousness and alluded to, hinted at, provoked as a place of deeper personal transgressive enjoyment. Even for those who have sex as they should, there is pleasure and pain when they follow this double contradictory injunction to conform to cultural codes and to go beyond them.

This is why psychoanalysis makes such a big deal about sex; people seek refuge in sex and puzzle over why it so often fails to bring them comfort. They are driven to it, and it drives them into the neurotic conditions that psychoanalysis was invented to treat. And, for those who do not have sex as they are told they should, they are haunted by a culture that is still always pressing on them the demand to conform to what is demanded of them, and that too drives them into the privatised suffering that psychoanalysis can help unlock.

Take, for example, the trading of sex for love which so often happens inside the nuclear family—implicit in the marriage contract—and the more explicit trading of sex for money when those with power, usually men, are able to use it in order to command others, usually women, to service their bodies, to give them enjoyment. On the one side of the equation is enjoyment, and on the other is suffering. Often they are combined. In this way, sex is turned into work, and commodified and exploited, as all work under capitalism is. The answer is not simply to prohibit this work, but to transform work as such, and that means fighting for sex workers to have rights, paving the way for a world in which such commodification and exploitation of sex would be impossible.

Psychoanalysis teaches us that the prohibition of anything, including sex, is not a solution, but rather that our task is of understanding structures of repression as such, and tackling those structures. With new structures that we collectively create for ourselves come new possibilities for desire, for desiring others, and new paths for the drives, paths in which the enjoyment of one does not require the humiliating suffering of others.

The drive feels as if it is inside us, but it is actually on the border of inside and outside; more correctly, as Freud himself declares, on the border of the physiological and the psychical. What is physiological is given shape and meaning by who we understand ourselves to be, and what we are told our needs and desires are; and the 'psychical' itself is, as we learn from Marx, as much outside us as inside us, our subjectivity being 'an ensemble of social relations'.

Those social relations are produced by the culture we ourselves create, but in an alienated society such as ours, we make our culture and our history in conditions that are not of our own choosing. What we must do, and what psychoanalysis guides us to be able to do, is to be able to comprehend the reality of the 'second nature' of our human nature, the second nature of culture.

History and culture shape and incessantly modify the realm of the drive. We need to be clear that this drive is not biologically wired in 'instinct', nor that there are separate biologically wired-in life and death instincts. There are indeed instinctual processes concerning food and sex and other biological needs that are a function of our deeper evolutionary history as an animal species, of our animal nature, but these are always interpreted by us, consciously or unconsciously.

That which drives our body, and which is as alienated as the bodies that we routinely treat as if they are mere vehicles to drive to work under capitalism, is always mediated, shaped by culture. There is no drive without culture. This is not actual 'instinct' which precedes culture, but something quintessentially human, as human as the cultures we create. We cannot free ourselves from culture in the name of our drives; much less liberate ourselves from our drives in favour of culture.

This is not the question raised by liberation movements. It is a false question leading us down false paths, to a mistaken idea of the drive as an instinctual force that must be 'released'. That makes it seem as if the unconscious is inside the head like steam in a cooker, and as if the drive will burst forth like steam. Instead of this false reductive ideological and fake-psychoanalytic question, our psychoanalysis is in tune with the question posed by the liberation movements. The question they pose is whether this culture should continue to benefit the 1%, allowing them to grab life and condemn the remaining 99% to mere survival and death, or whether we can now begin to create a culture in which everyone might live and flourish.

Interpretation

The drive is what results from the *interpretation* of instinct, from its alteration, complication and perversion as it passes through language, ideology, culture and history. We are concerned here with drive and its interpretation, the two linked together. Words transmute instinct into something that is no longer just biology and physiology. The drive is on the border of the physiological and the psychical. Its origin is in fantasy and not only in the body. It is not something given naturally, but a historical product. We maintain that fundamental premise of psychoanalysis against the ideological reframing of drive as something of unchanging human nature. Our humanity transforms the drive by the same gesture by which it transforms itself.

The drive is incessantly transformed under the determination of the symbolic, of signifiers, of culture. This does not mean that it is not real. Drive is also real; it overflows words, it cannot be contained or channelled by the symbolic, it resists any symbolization, it appears as an implacable force, outside the signifiers we use to make sense of what is happening to us.

Beyond any sense, the drive is itself a part of what is happening to us. It takes form in our lives, as life, when it is elaborated in language, in the signifiers that structure our speech and action. It is here a real effect of the symbolic. This real aspect of drive is what makes it appear in the body as if it were indeed an instinctual force, an imperative need for food or for sex. This real aspect of the drive also enables it to appear in our speech through disturbed, excessive, absurd or useless operations such as rituals, pet words, exaggerations, automatisms and repetitive signifiers in which we are subject to senseless ideological repetition, to ideology as a kind of machine.

Ideology is indeed rather like a machine. There is something mechanical, deadly, mortifying about it. It is a kind of manifestation of the death drive. It smothers what novelty there might be in repetition and turns creativity into something deadening. Ideology is dead life, the illusion of life whose aim is death. It is then that we see one of the faces of sex in this sick world, sex intimately linked to suffering as well as to enjoyment, the face of sex that posed questions about the nature of subjectivity under capitalism that psychoanalysis was developed to answer. So, once again, when we talk of drive we must talk about sex.

Sex

It is in drive that our biological needs, for *sex* among other things, are reconfigured as social needs. These needs are both created and expressed and repressed as a function of the structure of the family, private property and the state. Cultural and historical institutions do not simply exclude natural tendencies, but absorb, use and modify them, in addition to relying on them.

For example, when instinctual reproduction of the species underpins and is then informed by social or family institutional life, this biological process is turned into human sexuality, which is released from its reproductive anchor, as well as diversified and complicated at the level of drive. This is how eroticism can permeate consumption, advertising, the culture industries and charismatic leadership. Psychoanalysis shows that even scientific work, religious beliefs and political ideals involve idealized, sublimated or rationalized erotic elements.

Sex itself is transformed into one of the nodal points of society, as relay and rebellion against power. This is another reason why sex is central to psychoanalysis; sex operates as the historically-constituted symptomatic kernel of social relationships in class society. These relations of domination, but also of struggle and conflict, are articulated around and based on a sexual axis. Patriarchy is inseparable from capitalism. Consumerism and capitalist voracity reveal highly sexualized possessive tendencies.

No man is an island, but capitalism drives him to imagine that he is, and to imagine that the only way to love someone is to possess them. Women, who are so often reduced to the level of objects to be possessed by men, can also make the same mistake. As has been said by a wise communist novelist, liking is the best form of ownership and ownership is the worst form of liking.

Our sexuality is not only the most animal aspect of us, but also the most human, the most characteristic of our humanity. Human culture results from a certain cultural metabolism of sexuality. It is in their condition, as sexual and sexed beings, that human beings are social beings. Their socialization is a process whereby sexuality is symbolized, maintained and transcended symbolically, and it becomes word, part of language and so of desire, love, friendship, solidarity, social relationships, cultural institutions, political action and other symbolic practices animated by our desire.

There is no specific sexual drive, any more than there are separate pre-existing drives for life and for death, but the drive in this culture hooks into sex as something most personal and private and hidden about us. In this way, everyone is hooked into the culture of sex, whether they intend to avoid it or not, and into the sexualisation of commodities to make them more alluring, to make them sell more.

Our sexuality is instrumentalized by domination instead of being a means of liberation. Under these conditions, the psychoanalytic answer cannot simply be to demand more sex. That is a caricature of Freud's position, a caricature that has attracted some of the so-called 'Freudo-Marxists', those who have tried to radicalise psychoanalysis by making a combination of Freud and Marx that was sometimes, only sometimes, too-fast and simplistic.

As we have explained, the task is not to release pre-existing urges to make us happy, neither at the level of the individual in the psychoanalytic clinic nor at the level of the collective in political struggle. Rather, the task is to refuse what we are told to want, to create the conditions in which we might better choose what will be good for us all. Instead of simply demanding more sex, we need to work through how and why enjoyment becomes connected with suffering in sex, and how sex as a wellspring of life is turned against us, to function as if it were itself also part of the death drive. To turn the drive back towards life again, we need to articulate it with that most human of phenomena, desire.

Desire, of others

Desire is human because it is created in the ensemble of social relations that make each of us into human subjects. While drive can impel us to treat ourselves as the centre of the world, masters of nature, and takes on a repetitive and sometimes self-destructive form, desire is intimately connected with others. Desire has a peculiarly dialectical quality of being a desire for others and a desire that we are driven to obtain from others. The recognition that we desire from others binds us to them, and we seek in them something that pulls us towards them, to desire them.

This is the source of enjoyment and suffering in social relations, and it then also drives us to build culture as a shared medium, a symbolic medium through which we might share what we are with others, to participate in something that is other to us. This drive and pull operates at the level of interpersonal face-to-face relationships and at the level of organisations and the construction of shared ideals which bind a community together, including globally. It is the mainspring of individual sexual love in societies that have given value to that kind of desire, and of solidarity in the international networks that the liberation movements build. We reframe that solidarity here in order to draw attention to an aspect of it, not to colonise it with psychoanalysis. Our desire, political solidarity, is ideologically chained to sex under capitalism, and it is that aspect that psychoanalysis helps us to understand.

Drive is already transformed into desire in our distinctive forms of subjectivity. As speaking beings we are in a symbolic realm, a collective medium of communication, a shared space in which we become truly human. Here our desire for others is reflexively transformed into the most diverse and complex forms of relationship, which, though experienced as lying deep within us, are also conditioned by others, between us.

The symbolic realm, as something independent of us, can so easily and often turn into a machine-like force which is exacerbated by ideological repetition of alienating images of ourselves. Alienation and ideologization are two risks we must take when we symbolise sexuality. The cultural functioning of sexual need as if it were an implacable drive and an irrepressible desire is intimately bound up with ideological distortion, perversion of sexuality, bound up with alienated sexual relations that are structured symbolically in a way that allows not only for the reproduction of culture, but also for the perpetuation of relations of domination and destruction such as those prevailing in the capitalist system.

Markets

In capitalism, through ideologization and alienation, life is turned into death, death drive, and communication is turned into reification and commodification of human beings, human creative labour and human objects of desire. Things and commodities usurp the place of people and exercise powers and rights of people, such as that of free circulation, of which a large part of the world's population is deprived. In capitalism, especially in neoliberal capitalism, fetishized objects are more 'subjects' than human subjects themselves. Capitalism puts subjects at the service of objects. It puts the interests of the market before those of humanity. It makes the possessive, accumulative, competitive and destructive tendencies of capital govern and define human drives.

Alienated needs become the driving force of the market that encompasses everything under capitalism. This market includes sexuality. Gender grows into the poisonous site of forms of commodification, such as pornography under patriarchy, with women turned into objects to be bought and sold, to be owned and exploited, to be enjoyed and exchanged for money. There is little place here for desire, but only for the drive and for what appears as instinct, what appears ideologically to be mere animal instinct rather than something human.

The real reduction of desire to drive and then the ideological reduction of drive to instinct turn our creative human activity, our symbolically-mediated relation to others, into things that work in an objective, rigid, automatic and meaningless way. Our bodies, and parts of our bodies, are turned into alienated sites of dumb, deaf and blind biological processes which we fetishize or fear. Radical disability activists have thus drawn attention to the way that the 'deaf', 'dumb' and 'blind', operate as ideologically-loaded signifiers of beings less than human—sometimes even reduced to objects rather than being subjects—less than the 'normal' body we are told we should possess in order to work, to produce 'surplus value' for our employers.

These processes leave us out, exclude the subject, but produce the imaginary. It is as if communication of images of nature and the self could be relayed independently of symbolically-structured, historically-constituted social relations. It is also as if what we experience as an aspect of commonsense directly reflects what is real.

The market is today imposed as the only reality. Everything has to be commodified, sold, bought and exploited. This generalized commodification is characteristic of capitalism, but the production of commodified images of gender is also a function of patriarchy. Patriarchal power is decisive as well for the tendencies that capital imprints on our relations with things and people. Modern subjects, subjectivated by capitalism and patriarchy, relate to the world and others as competitively, possessively, accumulatively and destructively as the prototypical macho lover does with women. This is what drives the macho entrepreneur, and, unfortunately, sometimes the heroic activist leader in a social movement.

Machismo

We should not be surprised at the hyper-masculinized and misogynist element of the male model of the pro-capitalist neoliberal ultra-right. The current form of capitalism requires *machismo* as a subjective prerequisite. Fighting against this machismo and the other expressions of patriarchy is a way of subjectively undermining capital. It is for this, and for much more than this, that feminism constitutes a threat to current arrangements of power, which, now as before, mysteriously evoke what Freud represented through the mythical figure of the oppressive father of the primitive horde, projecting back into prehistory the patriarchal bourgeois nuclear family of modern capitalist society. It was a deeply ideological move, but it also now reveals something of the nature of sexualised macho bourgeois ideology.

Feminism not only threatens the subjective foundation of capitalism and the commodification of gender. It also endangers the personal-political ideological social bonds that structure the bourgeois nuclear family, insisting that these bonds are deceptive imaginary figurations of real human needs and reflection of symbolically-sanctioned oppression. This is why feminism, along with the broader lesbian, gay, bisexual, transgender, queer, intersex and associated struggles, is an indispensable ally of psychoanalysis in the service of liberation movements.

Psychoanalysis does not define how we should love and who we should love, nor does it specify what sex should be like or what kinds of bodies should have sex with other bodies. Drive and desire follow complicated paths which are singular to each subject, and a pressing political task is therefore to create multiple possible conditions in which those who have sex, or those who choose not to have sex, are able to define themselves and do what they decide. Psychoanalysis is not designed to attach people to what they have been told sex is, rather it is a practice of self-inquiry that enables us to change our relationship with any or every 'good' that is held out in front of us as bait.

Psychoanalysis can help us change our relationship with the world, either by reconsidering what surrounds us, dealing in a different way with our drives, or opening new spaces for our desire. All of this is crucial for liberation movements that must also change their relationship with the world they want to change. To achieve their goals, activists must profoundly transform their relationship with their immediate environment and also with other people, which they constantly try to do, from the beginning, by establishing horizontal relationships with each other, by experimenting with radical forms of democracy and by weaving networks of action and solidarity.

The liberation movements create networks of action to change the world and also, crucially, networks of solidarity that progressively expand their domain of action, to include those not directly involved, but all those who desire to be part of change in the world. Solidarity is love for those who are other, far away, as well as those who are close. It is symbolically effective, not merely imaginary. This is the space for the realisation of the drive in such a way that it becomes a force for the elaboration of social relations, and of a culture in which our desire for others is configured in such a way as to receive from others an acknowledgement and recognition that we are not mere animals, our bodies not mere machines, that we are human.

In this chapter we have focused on our intimate relationship with the realm of culture, and on the insights psychoanalysis provides into the nature of what drives us as human beings. Here psychoanalytic theory participates directly in the work of the liberation movements, learning from them and giving to them some additional conceptual tools to understand how culture works, how it can operate in a creative constructive way, and how it becomes perverted and turned into something as oppressive and destructive as capitalism.

In the next chapter we turn back to the psychoanalytic clinic, and we will elaborate our specific approach to the unconscious repetitive work of the drives, and how these are embedded in power relations. There is this power in the clinic because there is a peculiar constellation of power relations in this society. The psychoanalytic clinic is in this world, of this world that we so much want to change; it works through *transference*.

5

TRANSFERENCE: POWER, RESISTANCE AND ANALYSIS

The 'transfer' of structural phenomena concerning desire and power from one realm into another, *transference*, has a technical meaning and use in psychoanalysis. But beware, for structures, structured patterns of relationship, are replicated and repeated across the social field, and down into our organisations and into our families.

Psychoanalysis focuses on the way that personal relations with others, including relationships structured in the family, are transferred into the clinic, repeated in the signifiers the analysand uses to configure and comprehend their relationship, or lack of relationship, with their analyst. This reduced meaning, in which the transferred structural phenomena concern early love experiences repeated in relation to a psychoanalyst, is then also susceptible to an ideological generalization.

Psychoanalysts are often tempted to 'apply' their own particular understanding of transference in the clinic back out into other realms of social and political power relationships. Those relationships are thus clinically analysed, mystified and psychologized, ignoring the fact that they need particular analysis and action, political analysis and action which then help us better understand the nature of psychoanalytic treatment itself. The mistaken attempts to 'apply' psychoanalysis to realms outside the clinic occurs when the Freudian perspective turns into a worldview that pretends to encompass and understand everything; it then involves a vision of what society is and should be, and demands a particular kind of moral position, one that we reject.

The same temptation to 'apply' psychoanalysis happens when the treatment is generalized, when it goes beyond its field of competence, after having become a professional disciplinary speciality competing with, and adopting the language of, rival psy approaches, such as psychiatry, psychology and psychotherapy.

Psychoanalysis is really neither a worldview nor a specialized and then generalized discipline, but many practitioners are understandably lured into imagining that it should function as such by their own precarious claim to knowledge and expertise. These practitioners forget a fundamental principle of the treatment, which is that it is the analysand who analyses, that it is the analysand and not the psychoanalyst who has something significant to say about themselves.

Giving analysands a voice and acknowledging their place in what they say can have decisive, sometimes liberating effects on their lives and the kinds of relationships they establish with others. Similarly, there are oppressive logics that are reproduced when the psychoanalyst continues to speak instead of the subject. We need to focus now on the power of the clinic to bring to life certain kinds of relationship in order to work through them, the forms of resistance to this power. We need to focus on the role of psychoanalysis as a resource and ideological model for personal and social relationships, and this is something radical and potentially revolutionary psychoanalysts working with liberation movements need to be aware of.

Power, in and of the clinic

The clinic has power in this society because people seek refuge there, and they find in that place opportunity to speak in a way they have never spoken before. The analyst, as witness to their suffering and enjoyment, hears them speak, encourages them to speak, and so makes the unconscious more present to them. It is in the clinic that the analysand makes and hears connections between signifiers that they may never have made, heard and been moved by before. Even those who never go into the clinic suspect that something strange is happening there. Sometimes they feel threatened by what is spoken about, especially if someone close to them is speaking, and may be speaking about them to another, to the psychoanalyst. Sometimes, the clinic as a private space for speaking private thoughts is viewed as a threat by those in power who would like total knowledge and control over what their subjects are saying.

The power of the clinic, a potentially subversive power, can be abused, and so the task of radical psychoanalysis is to protect that space and articulate its radical potential with liberation instead of oppression. The first and the least that this task requires of psychoanalysts is that they refrain from persuading, suggesting or manipulating the analysand. This in turn requires extreme caution and a good deal of silence.

The psychoanalyst is mostly silent, and does not pretend to know exactly what their analysand's words mean. The power of the psychoanalyst in the clinic is concerned with the boundaries that define that peculiar space, with what is transferred into it at every moment and with the opportunity to make the border between consciousness and the unconscious more visible to the analysand. Their task should not be concerned with divining what lies inside the unconscious, as if they were simply opening a box in the mind, and much less with advising the analysand on the basis of supposed knowledge. The psychoanalyst has knowledge about the nature of language, but not about the specific singular way that their analysand is using their own signifiers to structure their own fantasy and their own relationships with others.

Objectivity

Words in the clinic cannot be clarified, understood and answered with a supposed knowledge of psychoanalysis as it would be with the supposedly objective scientific knowledge of psychology or psychiatry. *Objectivity* is very different in this peculiar realm of the clinic where subjectivity is a necessary ingredient. The mainstream psy professions cling onto a fake image of science, and then attempt to implement that image of science in their work with human beings. These professions, and professionals separated from those they treat, make a double mistake, first in their mistaken idea about natural science and second in their attempt to enforce it in their own clinical work.

It is in the nature of our reflexive divided subjectivity as human beings that 'objectivity' does not exclude subjectivity, is *not* the opposite of subjectivity, as if it were a zero-sum game. Here is another key lesson of psychoanalysis that is relevant to every theory of liberation as well as to our own practice in the clinic. The false ideal of 'objectivity' that the mainstream psy professions try to attain is actually an expression of the subjective sphere from which they cannot escape. It is a version of subjectivity, but an alienated, unconscious version. It is a peculiar distorted form of subjectivity that does not recognise itself as such. They try to escape it, and fail.

What the traditional psy professionals think of as their 'objectivity', their supposedly neutral, distanced stance towards those in distress, is nothing of the kind. It is actually suffused with subjectivity, structured by their particular position and experience, position and experience that they refuse to take into account. The stance they take when they treat people like objects, as if they are mechanisms that can be 'treated', is of a master in command of all the knowledge that is necessary, knowledge that their poor patients know nothing of. Psy treatment itself is not only something impersonal based on objective knowledge, but already involves two personal links that embroil drives, enjoyment and desire; a subjective relationship of professionals with purportedly objective knowledge and a power relationship of professionals who do think of themselves as subjects working on their patients as objects.

Subjectivity internally constitutes the objectivity of the supposed knowledge of psy professionals. And so, these 'objective' practitioners feel all the more threatened when psychoanalysis points out that their mastery is fragile, and that they too are divided subjects. Psychoanalysis shows us how we always operate in relation to knowledge, never in complete command of it, and that this relation to knowledge needs to be grasped as a form of subjectivity. It is into that relation to knowledge that we pour our hopes and fears, our sense of alienation, and our ability to speak and to listen to others who speak to us in the clinic.

Unlike psychiatrists and psychologists, the psychoanalyst does not have any special knowledge about the singular subject who speaks to them in the clinic, and should not pretend to do so. This speaking being they listen to is a subject and not an object, not an object of knowledge. The psychoanalyst must deprive themselves of any claim to knowledge about the analysands as well as of any desire for power over them. The first desire for power that must be renounced in psychoanalytic practice is precisely one inherent in their supposed knowledge, knowledge supposed by their analysands, the desire for instruction, persuasion and suggestion.

Analysands should not be convinced or deliberately manipulated and dominated by the psychoanalyst as they are daily by psychiatrists, psychologists, psychotherapists, parents, friends, colleagues, bosses, teachers, evangelists, ideologues, intellectuals, politicians, journalists, publicists, entrepreneurs or advertisers.

Desire for power is found in all the fibres of this human society. It becomes a deathly drive among those who accumulate capital and among those who willingly, if unconsciously, turn themselves into commodities. It operates among racists who desire domination over others, and among those who willingly, if unconsciously, turn themselves into victims. And, in the liberation movements, desire for power operates among those seeking escape from exploitation and oppression in the bureaucratic apparatuses that then represent and speak for others instead of enabling people to speak for themselves. Such symbolically-structured forms of desire and power are questioned and challenged by the analysand in the psychoanalytic clinic.

Psychoanalysis opens a space in which power and the desire for power can be transferred and clinically treated. This is also why transference in the clinic is crucial. What is 'transferred' into the clinic and made experientially visible to the analysand; heard by them in the signifiers they use to structure an account of themselves, is the peculiar knotting of desire and power that has made them who they are inside the social structures into which they were born.

Families

Among the most potent of the symbolically-warranted social structures are *families*. In the modern Western, and now globalised version of this apparatus, the family is condensed into a mechanism with clearly distributed gender-stereotypical functions. This mechanism is the patriarchal nuclear structural matrix, which is powerful as a model form, a societal structure, not because it actually exists as such—though some people do indeed live inside a nuclear family consisting of a mother, a father and, perhaps, a brother and sister—but because it operates ideologically as a stereotypical normative structure.

This model form is held out as an ideal for people to aspire to, and to feel lacking if they are living in a household with no mother, or no father, or no siblings, or with carers and children to which they have no blood-tie. It seems as if all happy families are alike precisely because this image of the family is a potent mythical force, and so it is all the more sad to see some psychoanalysts treat it as an ideal in their theories of 'normal' or 'abnormal' developmental journeys through what they call the 'Oedipus' complex.

Oedipus, who in Greek theatre, was left for dead, and then, through a very strange set of circumstances, ended up unwittingly murdering his father and marrying his mother, lays down the matrix for a particular set of family relationships, and especially so among conservative psychoanalysts. This story, and those relationships, also lay down the basis for a drama of rivalry of the boy child with his father and his love for his mother, and if it is used as a normative model in the clinic, then it does, indeed, amount to a form of ideological 'Oedipalisation' of psychoanalysis. What happens to girls is viewed as a mystery, and conservative psychoanalysts treat femininity, at best, as something mysterious, a 'dark continent', and at worst, as a simple object, as part of the scene of the Oedipal drama of masculinity.

Enough of that, for most psychoanalysts have moved beyond that, recognise the limitations of this model of the family, and we liberation activists have to encourage them, help them break from familial ideology altogether. What we can do is to insist that this matrix sets up powerful ideals with which people identify, and so the clinical work must include tackling the way those ideals often structure the unconscious fantasy that people have about the nature of sexual enjoyment and suffering. It is that matrix that is often brought to life again in the clinic in transference, and psychoanalytic work enables us to move beyond that. Our psychoanalysis aims for another world, something different rather than the same.

The problem is that the same comes back again and again. The Oedipal nuclear patriarchal matrix becomes the emotionally-invested model for political-economic structures, which are then addressed in psychoanalysis and seem to confirm the Oedipus complex, which is logical, since they are inextricably linked with its ideological matrix. They can be 'worked through' though never completely left behind in the clinic. Dismantling and overcoming them is a task of liberation movements.

This is a problem posed by transference, for the peculiar forms of power condensed in the relation between analysand and analyst inside the clinic can then very easily be 'transferred' out again when the analysand leaves their analysis. This kind of 'transfer' happens each time an analysand leaves a session, and then may continue to experience relationships in the world outside the clinic in similar ways to those that have been constructed in relation to their analyst.

This kind of transfer sometimes happens when the analysis is completed, even when it has been successful in enabling the analysand to live a life without so much distress. It is then that analysands may come to idealise the transference, and continue to look for it everywhere, want to evangelise about psychoanalysis as if it were an effective means for everyone and everything. Here is a trap of the 'application' of psychoanalysis, but a trap that is all the deeper because it is based on an intense emotional experience, a lived relation, rather than just theory, rather than just the turning of psychoanalytic theory into a worldview.

The clinic in psychoanalysis can be so powerful because it is more than just putting theory into practice. The clinic is an experiential resonating container in which the psychoanalyst constructs the conditions for the treatment in such a way that they allow for the reproduction and condensation of the structural conditions in which the analysand's existence has been formed. The analysands are not only dealing with what happens in the treatment and speaking directly to the psychoanalyst, but also relate indirectly to what all this represents for them; a certain form is given to their understanding of their memories, their childhood, their family matrix and the political-economic structures which are formed in this matrix.

All this symbolic material is then inside the transference—the replication of the past inside the clinic —and constitutes the conditions for the analysand's treatment and speech, which are, as such, intimately connected with an intimately close bodily relationship.

The psychoanalytic clinic does not exclude the body and sexuality, and neither does it neglect the body's relation to structures and power because it opens a space for the subject to speak as they have never been able to speak before. Quite the reverse, for in fact these questions are central to psychoanalysis, for the individual subject lives out their pain and suffering, as well as their enjoyment through their body.

This suffering and enjoyment has a sexual dimension, whether or not it is deliberately enacted in the real world. It is enacted in fantasy, and it is this fantasy that is crystallised and spoken about in the analysis. Psychoanalysis provides a place where these matters can be put into language, and the subject can thereby work through in the transference how these matters have been constructed.

These sensitive issues, which are constantly enacted and suffered and silenced or mystified in everyday life, can be carefully addressed through attention to language by psychoanalysis. Here in the clinic desire is spoken about rather than simply enacted. Instead of being just lived and felt, it is contained, thought about and questioned. In this way the analysands hear and speak the truth of the relation they have forged between desire and power, the truth of their bodily relation to others, to other people and to social structures.

Fantasy

The encounter with desire and power in transference in the clinic as the replication of and reflection upon personal-political symbolic structures enables the analysands to encounter their unconscious and their unwitting interpretation of these structures at the level of *fantasy*. Again, and against caricatures of psychoanalysis which treat fantasy as a force bubbling up inside the head of the individual and then being contained by civilization, we insist that this fantasy is *constructed*. It is something elaborated by the subject, something internally organized, a kind of plot composed of signifiers that make sense and offer an interpretation of reality powered by desire.

Fantasy is a staging of desire that always includes a *subject*, defines who they are as divided in their enjoyment and suffering, and *objects* which they think, at an unconscious level, will bring satisfaction. Fantasy is a stage which, in transference in the clinic, includes the analyst as stand-in for these others and the objects that give a thrill and also cause anxiety to the subject. This is why the analyst is accorded power by the analysand in the transference, a power that is part of the fantasy, a replication of the power that has already held the subject in thrall.

Power in the psychoanalytic clinic is an effect of what happens in fantasy, of the staging of desire, but also of the attribution of knowledge to the analyst. The analysand supposes that the analyst has knowledge about them but, in the course of the analysis, discovers that they do not. This is something that also happens outside the clinic, in other life situations in which certain people, such as relatives, partners, charismatic theorists or political leaders, seem to have great knowledge about us and therefore also great power over our lives, at least before we are disappointed and free from them, when our fantasy dissipates. The difference in the clinic is that this transference, a 'transfer' of power, allows the analysand to reflect on and speak about what is happening at the very moment the relationship is being enacted in the signifiers they use to structure and speak about who they are.

The psychoanalytic clinic is a space to speak and think about fantasy instead of just living it. The internal link between symbolic structures and the subject, the subjective rooting of the structures, is thus revealed to the analysands. In this way the analysands come face to face with power and can speak their truth to power, the truth of their existence, of desire, while the analysts have an ethical responsibility to handle this desire, to direct the treatment, not to direct the analysands. This is power of a special kind. Power structured through the transference, brought to life in the clinic, must be handled carefully, with the release from this power coming from the accurate interpretation of it by the analysand.

We repeat, the analysis does not proceed through clever interpretations being given by the analyst. It is the analysand who analyses, and it is the analysand who interprets the transference. The analyst directs the treatment so the analysand can seize the power to direct themselves, to speak truth to power in psychoanalysis as the talking cure.

The analysts cannot respond directly to what the analysands expect of them. They must be absent and appear as a void in which the analysands elaborate what needs to be said. Although the analysts configure themselves as an object of desire, it is only as interlocutors, those who are spoken to about it. They sidestep desire, so that the analysand can notice better how it is being staged and what the consequences are. The analyst is able to utilise it in the transference and then to dissipate their presence there, to be discarded, annulled, forgotten. The analysts know that to allow fantasy to be enacted in reality instead of elaborated in speech would be abuse of power. To move too fast, to advocate a short-cut to action, would be to leave the analysand in the same place, subject to the same forms of power that led them into analysis in the first place.

The psychoanalyst eschews bodily contact precisely because that kind of gratification, gratifying perhaps at an immediate level for the analysand, destroys the analytic relationship. Sex in the place of analysis has a deadly double effect through which the transference is turned into a blind exercise of power and, as a consequence, the transference understood in psychoanalytic terms is also destroyed. Instead of releasing themselves from the transference through speech, the analysand then becomes trapped in a perverted version of the transference. The analyst as one who was accorded power, as one the analysand assumed unconsciously to know something about them in the depths of their being is really turned into a master, and the analyst who takes this fateful step beyond speech into bodily gratification is one who enjoys their mastery, mastery expressed through sex. This is a short-cut that knots enjoyment and suffering together instead of untying the bond between the two.

The repetition of forms of power and desire takes on an uncanny dimension through transference in the clinic. It is uncanny precisely because it combines two contradictory aspects of subjectivity; desire excited and repressed by power as well as power sustained and subverted by desire. Remember that desire is given form through the way it is prohibited, and that is one reason why the staging of desire in fantasy includes elements of anxiety and guilt as well as satisfaction through transgression.

It is in this sense also that power excites and represses desire, and desire sustains power and pretends to push beyond it. Power and desire, moreover, involve interactions between the political and the personal, as well as making manifest the separation, the gaps, the connections and the conflicts between consciousness and the unconscious. It is also for all this that transference in the clinic is uncanny.

Transference externalizes elements of personal-political relations in the analysand's existence, usually in the past and in their family, family relationships that have been repeated and can be consciously described to the psychoanalyst. It also brings to life unconscious elements that have been shut out of consciousness by repression, repression that bears upon what is so heavily invested with meaning under patriarchy, a form of sexual desire. This repressed and patriarchalized desire involves power, constantly makes itself present through being unconsciously repeated in the subject's life, and stains much of what they transfer into the clinic.

As the transference takes form in speech, in the signifiers that make it operate in the clinic, there is also the opportunity to track what is happening with desire. It is, at one moment, made conscious, and it still operates at an unconscious level. Fantasy is not dissolved in psychoanalysis, but we can come to know better what we, as analysands, are doing with it.

Truth

Not everything can be said, and the *truth* that emerges in the psychoanalytic clinic, the kind of subjective truth that is made possible by transference, is still divided between what is immediately momentarily conscious and what continues to operate unconsciously. The truth is 'half-said', but that is enough; that opens up new paths for desire. Transference is a trap and the opportunity for the escape from the trap it represents for the subject. It repeats the shape of past relationships precisely so that future relationships might be different.

Analysis links critique and change in a necessary transformative dialectical process through which understanding what is happening is simultaneously the moment when we are, by virtue of that understanding, doing something different. This is the case for political analysis and for psychoanalysis. Our existence can be transformed by the simple act of speaking and thinking about our symptoms, of interpreting them, of knowing something about the repressed truth that returns and makes us who we are.

Repression of sexuality, and the way sexuality is thus given shape for each individual subject by patriarchal social relations, are crucial for the clinic because they contribute to the disciplinary constitution of a specific type of subject characterized by certain kinds of symptoms, problems, sufferings and forms of amnesia, of things forgotten and half-remembered and repeated. The repressive and patriarchal normalization of desire enables a certain subjectification by enabling the domestication, domination and exploitation of people and their needs under capitalism, as well as their acceptance of forms of order as arbitrary as those of racism and coloniality. All this may be as conscious in its manifestations as unconscious in its causes and logics.

We can become conscious of the unconscious aspect of subjectification through the transference of key forms of our personal existence into the psychoanalytic clinic, but also directly through our social existence, for example by participating in liberation movements and in other transformative practices that function 'clinically' in modern society. Many transformative practices operate clinically, as they do in the clinic, not only psychoanalytic ones, and not always inside the clinic.

Resistance, in and of the clinic

The clinic is a site for the reproduction of power relations, but psychoanalysis conceptualises those power relations as transference, and so we know that our own best attempts, as psy professionals, to 'interpret' that power in the form of transference or to wish it away too fast will come to grief, will fail. Instead, as psychoanalysts, we direct the treatment, and only use our power to direct it, precisely in order that the analysand may speak truth to power. The analysand must be the one who speaks within the transference so they may better be able to dissolve its power, very much as the liberation movements cannot be handed power but must seize it for themselves. Both liberation movements and the analysand can only achieve their mission by knowing by themselves and for themselves what they are doing. The process of understanding the world simultaneously transforms it if that understanding and self-understanding is true.

The power of transference in the psychoanalytic clinic gives subjective shape to power in such a way as to undo it. It is in this sense that it is true that where there is power there is resistance. This means that it is necessary to grasp the nature of resistance both inside the clinic and outside it.

Clinic

What is a *clinic?* The 'clinic' operates not only inside the material architecture of the consulting room, but has a symbolic dimension of existence outside it by virtue of the spread of psychoanalytic discourse in contemporary society. This gives a peculiar prestige to psychoanalysis among those who can pay for treatment, and it evokes suspicion, for good reason, among those who cannot. The knowledge and power attributed to psychoanalysis can be discussed or rejected, but also monopolized and used, suffered and envied, adulterated and vulgarized, as well as distributed and democratized or subverted and transformed into something completely different.

Knowledge and power are part of the ideological and cultural wealth that is at stake in class struggles and other collective attempts to liberate ourselves.

We need to be clear that the peculiar power of transference in the clinic, the re-creation of a sense of dependency on the part of the analysand through the voicing of the particular signifiers they use to reflect upon the presence of the analyst to whom they speak, is utilised by psychoanalysts who direct the treatment, but this transference effect is not only confined to the psychoanalytic clinic.

Such is the impact of psychoanalytic discourse globally that many other forms of healing, whether physical or psychical, medical or spiritual, are affected by the kinds of knowledge that are attributed to psychoanalysts by their analysands. This supposed knowledge, which in psychoanalysis exists only to dissolve itself, is the main foundation of the authority and prestige of many physicians and psy professionals.

Transference was, after all, not invented wholesale by Freud, but conceptualised and utilised by him, and progressive psychoanalysts know how to use it in such a way that it can also be dissolved. Psychoanalysis always draws on an already existing kind of transference power, the effect of the replication of power relations condensed in a small space in relation to one other figure, but channels it in a particular way. Psychoanalysis is grounded in existing historically constituted practices from within religious traditions and from shamanic healing, and, of course, from the power of the medical doctor to provide almost magical cures to physical ills.

Unlike other practices, psychoanalysis must take a particular responsibility to handle the transference well, and to ensure that the paths out of it are as clearly elaborated as the paths into it. They may not be clearly elaborated for the analysand, they could not be because they are unconscious of it, but they are clearly elaborated for the psychoanalyst as part of their knowledge about social structure and language that are absorbed during training. Our articulation of psychoanalysis with the theory and practice of the liberation movements also means that we should extend Freud's own specifications for the training of psychoanalysts to include an analysis of power, and of the place of the clinic within existing apparatuses of power.

Freud himself was clear that alongside basic medical and 'psychological' knowledge, the most important requirements in psychoanalytic training were knowledge of history and literature, this all the better to enable the analyst to ground their work in their own culture, and in the culture of the analysand. Psychoanalysts today also need a basic grounding in the principles of political liberation. It is only that which will allow them to recognise the difference between their power to direct the treatment within the transference and their position within regimes of social power that accord their clinic some privileged status in some cultures.

This also means that psychoanalysts should acknowledge that there are many other forms of practice, political and even spiritual, in which subjectivity is reflected upon and transformed. Far from evangelising for psychoanalysis as if it were a worldview, and as if it were the only route to personal salvation, psychoanalysis must recognise that it is but one of many different kinds of practice that harness power, and that do so in ways that are cognate with 'transference'. The difference, the critical difference that marks out psychoanalysis from most other forms of care is that we analyse power at the same time as we use it to analyse subjectivity, or rather that we psychoanalysts use power to direct treatment in a way that allows the analysand to interpret and thus to analyse power.

Structurelessness

If we do not analyse structures of power we will be condemned to repeat them, and there is a connection here with the feminist argument that wishing away power, pretending that structural inequalities do not exist inside revolutionary organisations and social movements, simply gives licence for those with power to continue enjoying it, but in a hidden way. The illusion of *structurelessness*, the so-called 'tyranny of structurelessness' in political analysis, for example, is one way of naming the fact that attempts to pretend that a group is free of power, power structured along lines of gender, say, is just one more opportunity for men to retain control and for women to be silenced when they try to point out that there is something wrong.

The handling of the transference, and the insistence that it should not, as a rule, be 'interpreted' by the analyst, but that the treatment should be facilitated in such a way as to enable the analysand themselves to notice it, interpret it and so rebel against it, also connects with a basic principle of feminist organisation. This principle is summed up in the term 'standpoint'; the standpoint of the analyst as one with power is a standpoint that tends to overlook privilege and status and structure, whereas the standpoint of the analysand as the one who is subjected to power in the transference is one that allows, even incites them, to become aware of it.

It is this sensitivity to standpoint—enabling the subject to speak from their own standpoint rather from ideological knowledge of them or position accorded to them by others—rather than any sexist caricature of women, that leads the analyst to aim to 'hystericise' the analysand. Yes, women complain about their position, and have good reason to, and are then pathologised for that. They see something about the world from their position of powerlessness. Hysterical protest, whether by women or men, has been pathologised for too long, and it is psychoanalysis that does it justice. This hystericisation is a progressive incitement to complain, rebel, localise their complaint and understand better how their complaint in the transference is a form of 'conscientisation'; the analysand in this way becomes conscious of structures of power that operated unconsciously and repetitively, that drove their lives outside the clinic.

Hystericisation in psychoanalysis makes possible a kind of awareness such as that sought by liberation movements. These movements also 'hystericise' people in some way by allowing them to express themselves and be heard, which in turn helps them to become aware of the power that oppresses them, to deepen what has traditionally been called 'class consciousness' and to develop their spirit of protest and rebellion. Hysteria is not a disorder here, but an experience of truth and the only logical and sensible response to power. This means that psychoanalysis, which arises from the hysterical word and still cultivates it in its practice, can be of additional interest and use for our struggles alongside and inside liberation movements.

We fight for the control not only of the biological and technological-economic means of production and reproduction of life, but also of the symbolic means of expression and relationship, of existence and experience, of consciousness and desire, of knowledge and power. These means can either be privatized or socialized, ideologized or deideologized, used for domination and manipulation or for resistance and liberation. This is the case of the clinic in psychoanalysis, which has therefore constantly oscillated between its disruptive, subversive impetus, and its deviations towards adaptation, normalization and psychologization.

The psychoanalytic clinic is contradictory, and it is psychoanalysis as a dialectical practice, attuned to its own contradictions, that is best equipped to handle that. The contradictions of psychoanalysis are, however, the contradictions of society. The clinic of psychoanalysis is not outside our historically determined society. It is part of this society and its contradictions. There is then a structured discursive-practical frame to the 'clinic' as a form of social relationship that can be constituted and reproduced alongside other movements for liberation. Transference can be a way of intensifying the privatisation of distress or of connecting treatment with political resistance.

Whether used conservatively or in the service of revolution, transference presupposes the repetition of symbolic structures inseparable from capital, patriarchy, coloniality and other oppressive powers. These structures are what are repeated in the clinic. They are thus what reproduces the ideas, feelings, personal assigned roles and interpersonal relationships that are transferred into the clinic.

Analysis, of power and resistance

Transference allows us to recognize structure and then question or ratify it, distend it or reinforce it, expand or contract resistance to it, and so we can fight or resign ourselves to what is repeated. It is possible to act in one way or another in the structure. What we cannot do is to get rid of it once and for all, definitively free ourselves from what oppresses us, never repeat it again and move on a totally new and clear path.

The past is never completely behind us. We are always stuck in it and we must go through it incessantly to continue moving forward. This is why psychoanalytic treatment, although terminable, is also an interminable process that continues after the termination of the treatment. That is also why a revolutionary process fails when it thinks it ends with one simple political victory.

The revolution can and should be cultural and permanent because structural repetition does not cease and is inseparable from human culture. This is one of the reasons why Freud considered the unease in culture, discontent in civilization, to be insurmountable. We know that it has not been overcome, although some, including many psychologists, believe otherwise and want to make us share their brave new world, peddling us the illusion that we can be 'happy', while adapting people to this miserable world as if it were simply a case of slotting back objects into their environment, leaving it as it is, allowing it to continue to destroy itself until it disappears in climate chaos hell.

It is tempting to imagine that we live in a civilization without discontent, in a present that is no longer blocked and trapped in the past, in a life that has already ceased to constantly perform the repetition of a symbolic structure that the phenomenon of transference in psychoanalysis names and works with. This illusion is even more tempting among those who benefit from it and therefore ensure its operation in the present and through ideological images of its past and future, as if things could be always the same, as if there was no escape. We refer here to those who have power and exercise a power that imposes a surplus of repression on us, a power that adds avoidable discontent to our inevitable discontent in civilization, a power that is threatened by those who undermine it when they denounce discontent and speak of desire.

Those subject to power are the subjects who notice its operations. Here 'standpoint' in feminist politics gives voice to what we speak of in psychoanalysis, enabling us better to counter the 'tyranny of structurelessness', the illusion that there is pure unmediated 'communication', imaginary ideological evasion of political contradiction. There is always structure, in everyday life, in the clinic and in politics.

We are in the symbolic structure and we are condemned to deal with it. Transference is just one way to deal with it in the narrow particular domain of the psychoanalytic clinic. In this very limited space, transference makes it possible to condense, harness and 'work through' the structural repetition of signifiers and behavioural patterns in the life of an individual.

So, the subject can free themselves to some degree with psychoanalysis, but not only with psychoanalysis, and never with psychoanalysis alone. That is always insufficient in itself in its liberating power. It is true that working through the transference in the clinic conceptualised as a peculiar singular knotting together of power and desire opens the space for limited freedom

of speech and movement. But the potential for this freedom opened up by the clinic can only be realised outside
the clinic, in personal-political activity, when what is private becomes public, collective, and truly transformative,
subject to *action*.

6

SUBJECTIVE TRANSFORMATION:
TIME FOR UNDERSTANDING
AND MOMENTS FOR ACTION

We live in a world that is now structured like a gigantic globalised market-place, one that has given rise to forms of psychoanalytic theory and practice that are themselves privatized, commodified, turned into an expensive private treatment available to a limited few, only to those who can afford it. This should not surprise us in a capitalist society where every theory and practice of liberation has, at one moment or another, been turned into an academic commodity, distorted and turned against the social movements. Just as we need to rescue various currents of critical thinking from their confinement in universities and bookshops, so it is also necessary to remember what psychoanalysis was at its origins, to grasp what is true about it and not to let those with power rob us of its liberating potential as critical psychology.

We live in a world where psychoanalysis is necessary but impossible. It is usually realized in such a way that it is impoverished and disfigured to the point of being reversed. In the end it is then much less and even the opposite of what it could have been. Instead of being a revolutionary theory and practice, it is reduced to being an adaptive technique. Furthermore, it is confined to the individual and degenerates into a private practice marked by its conservatism, a relay point for reactionary ideas about sex and gender and much more.

In present-day privatised conservative forms of psychoanalysis, the four key phenomena we have described in this manifesto are distorted, turned into obstacles instead of opportunities. The unconscious, the unspoken ground of our collective being, is alienated in such a way as to turn into a threat and to privilege individual conscious instrumental reason. Our capacity to repeat action in different contexts with different results is turned from being a source of reflective freedom into the neurotic prison of the repetition compulsion. What drives us in our creative lives is turned against us in a machine-like force, subjecting us to the death drive. And transference is isolated in the clinic and, instead of showing us how social power works, is turned into a model for dependent relationships in the outside world. All of this has absolutely nothing to do with psychoanalysis. It does not display its reality, but only its impossibility.

The conditions of impossibility of psychoanalysis, in fact, are not only intrinsic; they lie not only inside it, in its disfigurements and inversions. Even disfigured and inverted, psychoanalysis is impossible for those who lack the financial resources to pay for it, for those who must work all the time and do not have even a few minutes to think about desire and for those who suffer from alienation that makes them disinterested in their existence and in their discontent in civilization.

More than that, psychoanalytic treatment is also somehow impossible for those who can easily buy it, consume it and in the end discard it just like another commodity, like any other luxury item, like a hobby among others, such as tennis, golf, yacht, yoga, Feng shui, charity, and art collections. And psychoanalysis is also made impossible, finally, for many people, particularly by those in liberation movements, whose sensitivity prevents them from accepting the commodification of the practice of someone trained and paid for listening to alienated speech and the fetish for payment elaborated as self-justification for the exercise of professional expertise, symbolic status and power.

Our task in this manifesto for psychoanalysis as the most radical possible form of 'critical psychology' is precisely to make it possible for liberation movements. More precisely, our task is to locate psychoanalytic practice in history so that we might connect it with the necessary progressive work of the liberation movements, and to combat the false futures promised by the adaptive psy professions. We need to treat psychoanalysis in the clinic as a transitional space, and turn psychoanalysis towards human liberation; instead of being an attempt to insert individuals back into this wretched society, we need to turn it into a conceptual and practical transition to communism. Part of that task is to retrieve from past struggles around subjectivity the historically progressive theory and practice of psychoanalysts who did concern themselves with misery precisely because many of them wanted to change the world.

History and revolutionary time

Psychoanalysis is at the edge of the psy professions, and often confused with psychiatry, psychology and psychotherapy by many people searching for answers, for the reasons for their distress and a way out. Psychoanalysis is actually something radically different. It is not actually a psy profession at all, but potentially a theory and practice of liberation. This means that it is crucial that we differentiate radical psychoanalysis allied with the liberation movements from psychiatric psychoanalysis, psychological psychoanalysis and psychotherapeutic psychoanalysis.

The best way of differentiating it from those false friends is through historical analysis. This analysis is, moreover, consistent with psychoanalytic radicalism. As we will see, authentic radical psychoanalysis is itself a form of historical analysis that turns to the past precisely to be able to orient us individually and collectively to the future.

We must include in our psychoanalytic work sustained focus on the repressed historical memory of our practice, on the radical history of the Freudian left, on the alliances of psychoanalysis with the socialist movement. We cannot forget the revolutionary pedagogical experiences of Marxist and Freudian inspiration in Austria and in the Soviet Union, the contribution of psychoanalysis to the Western cultural-political uprisings allied with the anti-colonial revolution in Indo-China in the second half of the twentieth century, and the commitment and persecution of psychoanalysts in Argentina and other countries. We must remember the free psychoanalytic clinics in continental Europe and acknowledge the free psychoanalysis offered now in the streets and public squares of Brazil. We must enable transference to operate again as something authentically psychoanalytic rather than as a manifestation of dependence induced by payment to one who pretends to know what we think we know ilies inside the unconscious.

These movements were, unsurprisingly, also accompanied by the so-called 'anti-psychiatry' movement. This was because many radicals recognised that psychiatry was a practice of medical mastery that turned people into patients, slaves of the mind-doctors in the old asylums, subjecting them to confinement and atrocious physical treatments. Psychiatry was attacked, quite rightly, because it was an obviously brutalising practice. Even though modern psychiatry looked to chemical cures in order to adapt people to capitalism, it actually continued a discourse and practice of feudal pre-capitalist masters. These kind of autocratic masters adapted themselves to capitalism while repeating the worst classical patriarchal sexist abuse of women and colonial racist persecution of indigenous people.

Psychiatry was a powerful tool in their arsenal. Psychiatrists were unscrupulous about putting themselves at the service of those who dominated, pathologizing people for their class, race, culture, gender or political position, torturing them and experimenting with them. When Freud, a psychiatrist, invented psychoanalysis, he had to break from psychiatry. That was a significant historical break that has to be repeated again and again to be effective today in anti-capitalist, feminist and anti-colonial struggle.

Psychiatry develops thanks to the impossibility of psychoanalysis. This impossibility is covered over and replicated in the medical psychiatric reframing of treatment in which different aspects of our distress are separated into discrete elements specified as different kinds of pathology. Medical and psychiatric diagnosis divides us by enclosing each one in their illness and by making us forget the common origin of what happens to us in this society. We are made ill by this political-economic system, by capitalism, patriarchy and colonialism. This sad world where we have no choice but to live today is now what we suffer when we become depressed or distressed, when we feel empty or persecuted, when we hear voices that others do not hear, when we are not able to work or concentrate on anything or relate in a progressive constructive way to others.

Illness

We need to treat our *illness* as a symptom of the lives we lead, not as indications of personal pathology. This kind of distress, however severe, is very different from the real physical problems that medical doctors treat. We are not the problem. Our 'illness'— and we borrow the term here as a metaphor for our distress—is only a sign and can also be a remedy against the real problem.

We need to turn this illness of the subject into a weapon, to speak of it as a weapon against power, to work through it as we speak of our desire for another world and act collectively on that desire. This is what psychoanalysis would make possible if it had not become impossible itself, if it had not degraded as much as it has, if it had not become another instrument of suggestion, ideologization, evasion of the world, seclusion in individuality, psychologization, psychopathologization, avoidance of conflict, adaptation and regulation at the service of the social reproduction of the existing world. In fact, it is psychoanalysis that, of all the psy approaches to subjectivity, is best able to appreciate the role of 'social reproduction' in the material replication of colonial and familial structures in the service of capital.

The impossibility of psychoanalysis in these conditions of pervasive racism, heterosexism and repetitive
demeaning of those excluded from power is intensified
by the reduction of distress to the level of the individual. The individual sphere, increasingly impotent, poor
and narrow, gathers force on the collective field and
ends up becoming the place where all the negative effects caused in our subjectivity by the capitalist process
of oppression and destruction must be resolved. Here,
though, diverse forms of psychology, including forms of
psychoanalytic psychology, operate alongside medical
psychiatric psychoanalysis.

It is true that psychiatry is often rejected by
psychologists who consider themselves to be more em-
pathetic, sensitive, thoughtful and respectful of the human being than psychiatrists, and who are quite aware
of the complicity between medicine and capitalism, as
evidenced, for example, in the power of the pharmaceu-
tical industry and in the fulfilment of the task of rehabil-
itation of the workforce by chemical means. Psychology
then pretends to replace psychiatry which operated as
a more obvious replicator of pre-capitalist relations of
professional mastery and servitude in which those who
suffer are treated as 'patients'. But this more modern psychology, which then arrogates to itself psychoanalytic
theory the better to inform quick adaptive cognitive-be-
havioural treatments, thereby replicates capitalism as
such by serving it with greater efficiency and speed, by
adapting us to it, by making it bearable, by preventing it
from being disturbed by our illness, by rehabilitating us
as workers and consumers.

Work and consumption, which are the main
functions of the human being for the production and realization of capital, should not necessarily be enabled by

psychoanalysis, whose subject is not that of capitalism. Not everyone needs to work all the time or to shop as a form of leisure. The subject that best suits capital is that of psychology, the more or less adapted and apparently free individual, the one who controls themselves, the best worker and consumer.

This 'healthy' subject of psychology is the symmetrical and inverse ideal reflection of the 'sick' subject in psychiatry. It is from the 'disease', by denying and mystifying the truth revealed by the disease, that 'health', a kind of normality, the pathological normality of capitalism, is conceived. This is why psychologists so often defer to psychiatrists as their real masters, and why psychological versions of psychoanalysis are as dangerous as psychiatric versions.

The subject of psychiatric pre-capitalist psychoanalysis, psychoanalysis harnessed to psychiatry, and capitalist psychological psychoanalysis, the adaptive version that is touted in the textbooks as a theory of mind and behaviour, is reduced to the alienated separate body or to the individual mind. In contrast, the subject of radical psychoanalysis, of psychoanalysis that is neither psychologized nor psychiatrized, is precisely the one which cannot be reduced to a mental or bodily existence. Our subject, the human subject, is not the alienated object of capitalist society, still less the slave-object treated by quasi-feudal colonial psychiatrists.

Our subject, as a *subject*, is externally related to these objects, to their alienation, to the mind and the body, to capitalism and colonialism. Our subject can be anti-capitalist and anti-colonial, and expresses its potential in the truth it speaks to power and potentially for a post-capitalist mode of being. It is that potential that is rendered almost impossible by current apparatuses of power. But history can also be made to speak, whether it is the history of the individual subject inside the clinic or the history of struggle that exposes the role of the psy professions in replicating instead of challenging power.

False futures promised by the therapeutic psy professions

Psychiatry promises to cure what it calls 'mental illness' and psychology promises to treat maladaptive thoughts and behaviour. Their practitioners who are trained in alienating practices, often struggle to find a voice for the oppressed, and some of those practitioners, such as those of the 'anti-psychiatry' movement half a century ago and of 'critical psychology' of the present-day, break from their discipline to join liberation movements.

One only has to think of the revolutionary psychiatrist Frantz Fanon who, when he joined the Algerian anti-colonial war after writing about white racism, continued working as a doctor with reactionary physical treatments of what he still thought of as 'mental illness', but then eventually put his energies full-time into liberation. Another striking case is that of Ignacio Martín-Baró, who criticized the psychological theories and practices of his time, proposing an alternative a 'liberation psychology' and fighting for the emancipation of Latin American peoples, especially the Salvadoran people, for which he was finally killed by an army death squad. It must be said that Martín-Baró sometimes used traditional psychological methods in his struggle, such as opinion polls, and he never stopped teaching and researching in the same field of psychology that he questioned.

Present-day 'critical psychologists' are caught in a similar contradiction, writing about the problems with their host discipline, but often continuing to be paid to teach in universities. The contradictions are brutally stark when these psy professionals are faced with realworld struggles for liberation.

Psychotherapy

It is here that our third false friend of the psy professions, *psychotherapy*, comes into the frame, an approach to distress with which psychoanalysis is often confused, and for good reasons because not only do many psychotherapists draw on versions of Freudian theory, but also many psychoanalysts for strategic reasons in the institutions that employ them call themselves psychotherapists, sometimes 'psychoanalytic psychotherapists' or 'psychodynamic counsellors'. The confusion is all the deeper because, in addition, it is true that the most radical forms of psychoanalysis do indeed have 'therapeutic effects'. These effects, however, are not the purpose of the psychoanalytic clinic. Its purpose, as we have seen, is a form of liberation and not simply an adaptive cure or a relief from conditions of oppression.

Psychoanalysis is not psychotherapy, but there is, nonetheless, something therapeutic about it. The difference between psychoanalysis and psychotherapy is that psychoanalysis deals with the contradictions of the subject, the world, and the subject in relation to the world. It is all the more important, then, to understand the way psychotherapy operates to smooth over the contradictory nature of this reality. Yes, it is true that there are some radical psychotherapists, just as there are some 'critical psychiatrists', but if they are really radical then they break in their practice from psychotherapy as such. The impossibility of conducting psychoanalysis today is one that psychotherapy pretends to salve, a problem it pretends to solve.

The psychotherapeutic technique can be functional for capitalism because it limits itself to fulfilling its task without asking more questions. It is an instance of the 'tyranny of structurelessness', promising a cure for distress in a world that is structurally-organised around alienation. That is, the pretence that there is no power, no structure, is the most effective ideological argument against those who suffer capitalism, racism, sexism and other forms of oppression, and quite rightly, complain about it.

The comforting reassuring insistence that there is no problem operates as a form of tyranny, silencing those who seek to change the world; they are told not to worry because it has already changed, is already all good, and the only problem is themselves. Psychotherapy is a fake, semblance of 'post-capitalism' and so, despite the best wishes of its practitioners in the psy professions, it often sabotages anti-capitalist struggle. Capitalism is not over, and so psychotherapy misleads us.

Alienation, structure and the other dimensions of power, which are at the centre of attention of psychoanalytic treatment, are usually presupposed and overlooked in psychotherapeutic techniques. Psychotherapy systematically evades the question of power, or, if it addresses power, it pretends to dissolve it in imaginary communicative relationships it constructs in its own form of clinic. These sentimental attitudes towards power are precisely those that best allow its exercise, sentiments that must be reactivated in transference in the clinic precisely so they can be worked through, overcome by psychoanalysis.

Just as psychoanalysis is a critique rather than a form of psychiatry and psychology, psychoanalysis is also, or should be, the diametric opposite of psychotherapy, including psychoanalytic psychotherapy which recuperates, absorbs and neutralises psychoanalytic notions. Psychoanalysis is not and cannot be a kind of psychotherapy. It does not exist to adapt or rehabilitate or cure the subject under the conditions established by capitalism. It cannot accept these conditions. It cannot be conditioned by them. This is also why it is not and cannot be confused with psychiatry, psychology or psychotherapy.

'Radical' psychotherapists and counsellors, who are often as critical of psychiatry and psychology as we are, will be unhappy with our claim that they too sabotage anti-capitalist struggle. And to a certain degree their discontent will be well founded. Although we have been harsh on psychotherapy, we must immediately, and dialectically, qualify our argument. The caveats are these:

First, that we readily acknowledge that psychoanalysis is itself compromised. Not every psychoanalyst is radical, and psychoanalysis has colluded with the oppression of women, with racist caricature, not to mention directly in torture for repressive regimes.

Second, more crucially, we repeat, psychoanalysis has therapeutic effects; it is not for nothing that many psychoanalysts also consider themselves to be psychotherapists. We admit that we could just as easily, or with difficulty, make the claim that psychoanalysis is 'radical psychotherapy' as we do that it is 'critical psychology' for liberation movements. Our radical psychotherapeutic friends unduly concerned with protecting their titles to practice would then need to break as thoroughly from their own host psy profession as critical psychologists will need to break from theirs.

Groups

It is with that caution that we turn to the question of *group* psychotherapy which, in the form of encounter groups and psychoanalytic work groups, and group analysis as a form of psychoanalysis, does appear to already operate as a more radical therapeutic practice. It is often viewed as more radical by political activists because it is more immediately 'collective', even if its collective aspect is still often confined to the space of the clinic and to sessions at a fixed time with participants who are treated as 'patients'. Group approaches have often been led by radicals, even by self-proclaimed Marxists, in parts of Latin America, and Group Analysis was founded by psychoanalysts and social theorists in Europe with a social theory of the psyche, by those practitioners who were very close to the 'critical theory' tradition.

The critical question for us is whether the exercise of psychoanalytic principles in groups necessarily mitigates or reproduces or exacerbates the problems of psychoanalysis in a society that individualises pain. It could be claimed that the kind of free association that is crucial to the psychoanalytic clinic is potentially more radical because group 'free floating discussion' gives the opportunity for many people to contribute and interpret what is going on. Forms of identification in groups can be turned in the direction of 'resonance' and so the transference is not channelled towards one figure, the analyst. Transference itself is experienced in a different way in groups because the multiple contradictory aspects of transference are present at the same time, present in different ways to different members of the group. Members of the analytic group work through their distress with other people rather than in a private space with one other person. After all, the group is thus a 'collective', and part of the cure is to learn to be collective rather than to be individual.

No matter how good arguments there are in favour of group approaches, they fail to convince us that these approaches are better than 'individual' psychoanalysis. We are not convinced, not because we are particularly suspicious of Group Analysis and other forms of group psychotherapy, but because our vision of radical psychoanalysis is not of it as focused on the individual, but on a form of subject that is as much collective as it is already located in one particular body. Psychoanalysis is always already in some way social and political.

We claim that although in the psychoanalytic clinic there is one person, an analysand, speaking to another, to the analyst, it is an illusion to conclude from that empirical image of the treatment that this is simply a two-body inter-individual practice. There are multiple subjects brought to life in the clinic through transference, and at an unconscious level many different subject positions activated in the speech of the analysand. It is not only the individual 'ego' of the analysand who speaks, but something beyond them, an unconscious world of contradictory subjectivities that are modelled on people who have been significant to them in their past, and they are speaking to many different figures who are present to them in the transference. The analysand is driven to repeat signifiers from the many different kinds of subject they have been, and they will open up possibilities for many other kinds of subjects to appear in the future, in the cure. There are therefore more than two people in the room in a psychoanalytic clinic; radical collectively-oriented psychoanalysis worth the name is a kind of group, already the most radical form of 'Group Analysis'.

This poses a radical task for us, which runs alongside the aim to make psychoanalysis something genuinely liberating, something allied to the liberation movements, rather than a conservative form of psychoanalytic psychotherapy. This radical task is a dialectical task. It is two-fold: we need to take group-analytic theory, which is radical, and make it genuinely psychoanalytic in our practice in the clinic; and we need to make psychoanalysis genuinely collective, opening it up to the group aspect of human existence, and taking it beyond that to collective subjectivity.

The future is collective, and it is through collective struggle that we will build a world that is a fully social alternative to the alienated individual existence that each of us suffers here now. We need to anticipate that world in our forms of struggle, and so psychoanalysis as a form of 'critical psychology' that breaks from all of the precepts of individualistic psychology also needs to anticipate in its practice the kind of subjectivity that will be a resource and driving force suited to that future.

It is true that the institutional practice of much psychoanalysis runs against the collective vision of the psychoanalytic subject that we have been elaborating in this manifesto. But there was once that collective vision, and there can be again. The 'testimonial clinics' and 'free clinics' that have been formed by psychoanalysts in recent years in Latin America redeem the radical past of Freud's free clinics in Europe before the Second World War. Again, it is the past that contains the keys to a radical future. What we must do is to turn present-day practice, with all of its contradictions into a transitional space, a practice that is geared theoretically and practically to the transition to a world beyond capitalism and colonialism and patriarchy. This other world is what we call 'communism'.

Transitions, in the world and in psychoanalysis

Psychoanalysis does not exist to serve the miserable world in which we live. That is why it is not really a psy profession at all and should not pretend to be, should not collude with psychotherapy, psychology or psychiatry in order to have status and power or recognition and acceptance. There is a marginal and transitional aspect to psychoanalysis that means that it has never really been well-adapted. Like the human subject it treats, psychoanalysis is 'dis-adapted', always failing to fit in, and challenging the society into which it was born. We need to intensify this transitional status with transitional demands of it articulated in alliance with liberation movements so that it is brought beyond what it is now, made what it truly can be.

Demands

Here we articulate four *demands*.

We insist, as our first demand, that the unconscious not be treated as a deep dark pit inside the individual, but as a collective resource for struggle and, more than that, the external place where we will have existed and acted as subjects. This means taking seriously the critique of the individual ego. We have to go beyond each one of us and find each other. The theoretical and practical resources for this are already in the unconscious, in the history that we carry with us, the buried memory of past struggles. This image of the deep dark pit is filled with racist imagery, and it betrays the collective struggle of black and indigenous people, as it does of women whose representation as obedient beings has not prevented them from being seen also as mysterious sites of unconsciousness and hysterical protest. Our demand is that no one, neither by gender nor by race nor by culture, be seen as unconscious or as the unconscious in contrast to the consciousness of the white, masculine and western ego. We also demand that the unconscious cease to be conceived in such a way as to allow sexist or racist caricatures. So this demand is simultaneously a feminist and anti-racist demand, a demand that we do not keep attempting to colonise the *unconscious*, but instead to allow it to speak.

Our second demand is directed explicitly to the clinic, to the clinical practice of psychoanalysis. The clinic can be an apparatus, a machine for the production of 'good citizens', as much as it can be the space for the radical unravelling of bourgeois, sexist and racist subjectivity. In this way it can ally with liberation movements and help them change the world, but it can also ally with power and neutralize any liberating gesture in the individual, changing the individual so as not to change the world. As a machine the clinic provides an instrument in which the drive that powers human action can too-easily be turned into a repetition of what is worst about that subjectivity, confirming it rather than challenging it. So, our second demand is that *repetition* in the clinic be treated as the opportunity for the construction of difference, something different rather than the same.

The third demand concerns the drive as such, and its place in the body as location of speech. We need to learn the lessons from Black feminism that it is silence that maintains oppression, a mute silence of the drive, and that the first step to liberation comes from willingness to speak truth to power. Yes, this is relevant in the clinic, but our demand is directed to psychoanalysts that they do not remain silent in the face of the power that accords them institutional power, prestige and privilege. Yes to the *drive* in speech, reflected upon and transformed. No to collusion with the idea that the analyst must be 'neutral' or 'objective' or pretend that they must be a silent partner in the political process. Speak out against abuse of power, including the abuse of power by psychoanalysts as well as other psy professionals.

Fourth, back to the clinic, to a critique and demand that *transference* in a clinical sense is not used as a model, not 'applied' by psychoanalysis to domains of social activity that they do not and cannot understand. Drop the pretence that you can tell us in the liberation movements what our struggle really means. Take seriously the key lesson from your own clinical practice of psychoanalysis, which is that it is the analysand who interprets, not the analyst. Transference is created in the clinic as a relay of power precisely so it can be undone again, and all efforts must be made to undo the power of the psychoanalyst when they are claiming to speak instead of the liberation movements.

As we have already made clear, in order to serve the liberation movements, psychoanalysis must clearly demarcate itself from psychiatry, psychology and psychotherapy. These three elements of the 'psy complex', the dense network of theories and practices about the human subject that warrants and reinforces power under capitalism and patriarchy, are now woven together in the global ideological process of 'psychologisation', expansion of the psychological at the expense of politics, society and culture, which are the places where we can meet each other to mobilize and liberate ourselves. Psychologisation, in its different competing contradictory aspects, reduces the most diverse cultural, social and political phenomena to psychological mechanisms, making us believe that each of us, as an individual, is responsible for causing and solving the distress endemic in this world.

Only collectively can we free ourselves. We must protect liberation movements from psychologization. We should not give them more psychology concealed under a psychoanalytic veneer. Nor should we forget that psychoanalysis, turned into psychology, has played a role complicit with the psychologisation of everyday life, including the psychologisation of political resistance.

To serve the liberation movements, psychoanalysis should not be a means to psychologize. It should not depoliticize the political by reducing it to the psychological, to the personality or to the inner world of the subjects, to their instincts, their complexes, their fantasy or their pathology. Nor should psychoanalysis funnel the responsibility of society into the individual or offer the romantic unrealistic image of an individual free of structures and capable of changing everything.

Freedom

We cannot promise total *freedom*. Such a claim made for psychoanalysis would be as fraudulent as those who imagine that there is a heaven without conflict or that everything will be like paradise on earth after revolution. Psychoanalysis can only be liberating by helping us to be aware of what prevents us from being free. This awareness is an immediate objective of the psychoanalytic method. Its fundamental technical rule of free association, for instance, is designed to make evident to the analysands what they cannot speak of, rather than produce the illusion that they could ever be free to say everything.

The rule of free association we are invited to follow inside the clinic also speaks of political desire. We speak about desire in the clinic so that we may speak about it outside, not so that we continue to carry the clinic around with us in everyday life, evangelising about it, but so that we can transcend it, move beyond the clinic, into politics. The field of politics is the only one in which psychoanalysis can end successfully, and also, without pretending to ever completely end, be a dialectical way of continuing critical analytic work by other means.

The subject of psychoanalysis is the one of politics. It is not the isolated individual, locked inside us, but each one of us working with others, inserted into who we are finding out who we are through our engagement with others. Here is the unconscious that can only be politics. This is the horizon of psychoanalysis.

The exploration of the unconscious leads us to politics. This radical process of politicization is the opposite of psychologization and makes use of psychoanalytical treatment in order to achieve the dialectical 'sublation' of it, leaving it behind while actually carrying it out; with it in order to transcend it. Technically understood, and this is a technical meaning that we need to import into psychoanalysis in order to radicalise it, sublation refers to a process that improves and transcends a given state of affairs while simultaneously cancelling out what it was that made what was offered by that state of affairs impossible. It is in the same way that the impossibility of psychoanalytic treatment can be overcome in liberation movements.

Such dialectical sublation of psychoanalysis requires an intimate link between what happens inside the clinic and what happens outside it, and then, only then, can we redeem the false promises made by other adaptive psy treatments. This is also how psychoanalytic treatment can take us out of it, lead us into the world and thus justify its existence. Psychoanalysis only makes sense when it takes us beyond it as such.

The most radical aim of this 'critical psychology' is not to keep psychoanalysis in place, but to relegate it to the past, to abolish the social conditions that have made it operate, to transform forms of subjectivity that call for psychoanalytic treatment. The ethical-political impulse is that another world is possible, a world in which we freely associate with each other and in which the free development of each is the condition for the free development of all. We aim to build a world in which psychoanalysis is possible but unnecessary.

BACKGROUND READING

We have deliberately avoided bibliographic references
so as not to dissolve our manifesto into the form of an
academic discussion, but we must recognize that we are
indebted to authors who have guided and inspired us.
There are too many and it would be impossible to mention them all now. We will refer below to just a few texts
we have found useful in working on this manifesto, and
you will find many ideas from them incorporated in and
reworked in it.

Psychoanalysis

This manifesto speaks of psychoanalysis in general, but
our work is influenced by a number of radical traditions.
We speak about Sigmund Freud, of course, and discuss
many of his ideas contained in texts such as *The Unconscious*, *Beyond the Pleasure Principle*, *The Ego and the Id*, and
Civilization and its Discontents. Freud's ideas are central
to any psychoanalytic work, conservative and radical.
There are many 'introductions' to psychoanalysis that
are misleading, in some cases quite wrong; a clear trust-
worthy introduction is *Freud: Theory of the Unconscious* by
Octave Mannoni.

The radical traditions that are important to us include psychoanalysts in the first wave of critical work around Freud, his followers who were also Marxists. In particular, we have learned from the work of Wilhelm Reich, whose fight for communism and sexual liberation caused him to be expelled from both the International Psychoanalytic Association and the Communist Party. Reich tried to use Freudian theory to understand the ideological rooting of society in the psyche, as well as sexual repression in capitalist society, and the way that repression was relayed through the bourgeois nuclear family into individuals, in books such as *Dialectical Materialism and Psychoanalysis* and *The Mass Psychology of Fascism*.

We also very much like the writings of Erich Fromm, who was a humanist psychoanalyst and a socialist deeply influenced by Marx. Fromm emphasized the way in which capitalism dehumanizes us, alienating us from our humanity, and encourages us to 'have' things which we believe will bring us happiness rather than to concern ourselves with 'being'. This is explored in his books such as *The Sane Society* and *The Anatomy of Human Destructiveness*.

Another key author for us has been Herbert Marcuse, who was an important figure for the liberation movements of the 1960s and 1970s. In his books *Eros and Civilization* and *One-Dimensional Man*, Marcuse taught us to appreciate the repressive aspect of certain forms of freedom in contemporary society. He has also helped us distinguish between the kind of repression that serves culture and the surplus-repression that serves oppression and exploitation under capitalism.

Later psychoanalysts who continued this radical tradition of work include Marie Langer and Joel Kovel.

Langer persisted at the end of her life to continue being a psychoanalyst without renouncing her participation in the liberation movements, as she explains in her text *Psychoanalysis and/or Social Revolution*. Kovel described clinical work in the the capitalist context, with lives affected by capitalism, in books like *The Age of Desire*. Kovel stopped practising as a psychoanalyst and became involved fulltime in Marxist and ecological politics as an 'ecosocialist', while Langer helped re-politicize psychoanalysis in Latin America.

The problem with so-called 'Freudo-Marxism' is that it is sometimes rather reductive; tending to see class structure as replicated directly in the character structure of individuals, and tending to make sexuality as it is conventionally understood in bourgeois society into an immediate experiential force for freedom. This is especially evident in Reich and to a lesser extent in Fromm, Kovel and Langer, but it was an idea and a problem already discussed by Marcuse. There is an excellent overview of these different traditions in Stephen Frosh's *The Politics of Psychoanalysis: An Introduction to Freudian and PostFreudian Theory*, and a very inspiring account of the way psychoanalysis was developed before the rise of fascism in Europe as a welfare-practice for all, not for private profit, in Elizabeth Danto's *Freud's Free Clinics: Psychoanalysis and Social Justice, 1918-1938*.

The tradition of work that has most influenced us, but one we are also critical of, is that of Jacques Lacan, a psychoanalyst who broke from the International Psychoanalytical Association to set up his own school to train analysts. Lacan shifted focus from biological forces and biologically wired-in stages of character development to language. Language organised through the Symbolic is more than just a medium of communication; it is a structure in which we occupy our place, an exteriority that surrounds us; it is 'Other' to us, as we explain in this book. We appreciate the critical work of Lacanian psychoanalysts on the history of its practice, for example Christian Dunker's book *The Structure and Constitution of the Psychoanalytic Clinic: Negativity and Conflict in Contemporary Practice*, and the attempts to connect Lacan directly with Marxism in the work of Samo Tomšič in *The Capitalist Unconscious*. We also appreciate the earlier theoretical intervention made in Slavoj Žižek's *The Sublime Object of Ideology*, as well as critical-theoretical appraisals of that work in Yannis Stavrakakis' *The Lacanian Left: Psychoanalysis, Theory, Politics*. Finally, we feel close to works that try to re-politicize Lacanian psychoanalysis in progressive leftist directions, whether moderate as in Jorge Alemán's *La Izquierda Lacaniana* or more radical such as Emiliano Exposto and Gabriel Rodríguez Varela's *El Goce del Capital*.

That Lacanian critical work would be incomplete and not viable without critiques from within the feminist and anti-colonial movements, critiques that are not always fully acknowledged. For us, the work of the psychoanalyst Juliet Mitchell in *Psychoanalysis and Feminism* was crucial for the argument that there were limitations to 'Freudo-Marxism' and that Lacan was worth taking seriously for linking personal change with social change. We have also been inspired by the psychoanalytic attempts to understand the embedding of racism inside both white and black subjects in the work of the revolutionary psychiatrist Frantz Fanon, particularly in his path-breaking *Black Skin, White Masks*.

Critical Psychology

We turned to psychoanalysis because although we were both trained in psychology, we came to see that there was something seriously wrong with that discipline, including its sexism, homophobia, racism, colonial functioning, complicity with capitalism and contempt for working-class people. The discipline of psychology sometimes uses psychoanalytic theory, usually in a reactionary way, and usually also abhors psychoanalysis, seeing it as a threat. Our argument in this book is that psychoanalysis is the most radical possible form of 'critical psychology', an attempt to turn around and treat psychology as part of the problem rather than as a solution to our ills.

Among the authors of 'critical psychology' who have most influenced us is Ignacio Martín-Baró, who connects the critique of psychology with a project of liberation. Martín-Baró insisted that psychology could only serve the liberation of the peoples of Latin America by liberating itself from its own alienation. We think that psychology can only free itself by freeing itself *from* itself. This is why we turn to psychoanalysis.

In the broad tradition of 'critical psychology' are psychoanalytic critiques, for example in the work of Néstor Braunstein who wrote, with Marcelo Pasternac, Gloria Benedito and Frida Saal, *Psicología: Ideología y Ciencia*. They show that the discipline of psychology pretends to be a science, but it is not, instead corresponding to an ideology and a technique at the service of capitalism. One of the most radical critiques of psychology today focuses on 'psychologisation' and the way that ideas from the discipline operate as a global force, in the work of Jan De Vos in, for example, *Psychologisation in Times of Globalisation*.

Not every critic of psychology looks to psychoanalysis as an alternative, and this is certainly the case inside psychiatry where the so-called 'anti-psychiatrists' and 'democratic psychiatrists' have often tended to see psychoanalysis as part of the 'psy complex', that is, as a 'psy' profession that aims to adapt people to society.

It is the internal critiques of psychiatry that have linked with radical politics that interests us most, of course, and these critiques include the work of Franco Basaglia in books like *Psychiatry Inside Out*, and Marius Romme, who wrote, with journalist partner Sandra Escher, *Accepting Voices*, which is about the phenomenon of 'hearing voices' as part of human experience instead of being seen as a pathological symptom of schizophrenia or a form of 'psychosis'. We have taken seriously the key phrase from Wolfgang Hüber's anti-psychiatric intervention *SPK: Turn Illness into a Weapon*.

We should also mention here critical Lacanian work on 'psychosis' by Annie G Rogers, a psychoanalyst who herself has lived with that diagnosis of 'psychotic' while continuing to practice, in *The Unsayable: The Hidden Language of Trauma*.

Politics

We come from different political traditions on the left. We include in this manifesto many ideas and even key terms and phrases from the work of Karl Marx, of course. Marx's ideas were crucial to the social movements that made the Russian and Chinese and Cuban revolutions possible, as well as many anti-colonial and anti-imperialist movements around the world. Marxism continues to inspire anti-capitalist and anti-fascist struggles throughout the world. We are with the radical spirit of these struggles and of the previous movements and revolutions, and with the defence of what was gained against the encroachment of bureaucracy, against the betrayal by self-appointed leaders.

Among the many critical Marxist writings that have influenced us are Ernest Mandel's *The Formation of the Economic Thought of Karl Marx*, which makes it clear that Marxism is a historically-specific analysis, an analysis of capitalism that aims to overthrow it, and his book *Power and Money: A Marxist Theory of Bureaucracy*, in which Mandel explains the collapse of the socialist countries by the disintegration of the political base of working-class power usurped by the bureaucracy.

We also acknowledge the contribution of Marx's co-worker Frederick Engels in *The Origin of the Family, Private Property and the State*. Although Engels was not a feminist, his interlinking of the institution of the family with the maintenance of private property and the kind of state structure that is dedicated to protect those with power in society is a scathing indictment of patriarchy. Feminist critiques of patriarchy have often, for very good reason, seen Freud as an enemy, for example Kate Millet's *Sexual Politics*. The most radical of the so-called 'second wave' feminism of the 1960s and 1970s then saw the appearance of socialist-feminist politics, and the slogan 'the personal is political'.

We are arguing for psychoanalysis in this manifesto, not taking our time to deal with the many critiques of it, though we do take seriously both feminist critiques and anti-colonial critiques, and critiques of the way psychoanalysis unconsciously reproduces the logic of social power, something masterfully elaborated in *Le psychanalysme* by the sociologist Robert Castel, and pathologises people who criticise it; that last issue is dealt with very well by the cultural anthropologist Ernest Gellner in *The Psychoanalytic Movement, or The Coming of Unreason*.

Socialist-feminist politics included anarchists, including Jo Freeman who wrote *The Tyranny of Structurelessness*, which we refer to in this manifesto. The different versions of intersection between radical political traditions are described and discussed in detail by Cinzia Arruzza in *Dangerous Liaisons: The Marriages and Divorces of Marxism and Feminism*. Black feminism in the work of Audre Lorde, for example in her book *Sister Outsider*, insists on the importance of speaking truth to power, an argument that we have referred to a number of times in this manifesto.

We have co-edited in Spanish a volume which includes many attempts by different writers to connect radical politics with critical psychology and psychoanalysis, *Marxismo, Psicología y Psicoanálisis*. This background reading is also available on these two blog pages, on which we have put links, where possible, to access key texts, and which also include articles related to the issues we cover here and updates on the manifesto: https://sujeto.hypotheses.org/ and https://fiimg.com/psychopolitics/.

THE AUTHORS

Ian Parker is a psychoanalyst working in Manchester in the north of England. He is a Marxist, and member of different left groups and campaigns. Much of his academic work has been concerned with writing and promoting versions of 'critical psychology', different ways of developing theoretical alternatives to mainstream psychology and practical initiatives to address human distress.

David Pavón-Cuéllar is a professor in the faculties of psychology and philosophy at the Universidad Michoacana de San Nicolás de Hidalgo, in the city of Morelia, state of Michoacán, Mexico. He is a Marxist and participates in radical Left collectives in Mexico. His academic work develops at the intersection of Lacanian psychoanalysis, Marxist theory, and critical psychology.

Suryia Nayak is a Black feminist activist, group analyst and senior lecturer in social work, putting intersectionality and psychoanalysis to work for collective liberation from oppression.